THE SECRETS OF TOFU

THE SECRETS OF TOFU

W. Foulsham & Co. Ltd.
London • New York • Toronto • Cape Town • Sydney

W. Foulsham & Company Limited
Yeovil Road, Slough, Berkshire,
SL1 4JH

ISBN 0-572-01383-3

Printed in Spain by Cayfosa, Barcelona
Dep. leg. B-27224-1986

CONTENTS

ABOUT THE AUTHORS

Jean Conil was Executive Chef at the Arts Club in London until his retirement in March 1986. He is also principal of the Jean Conil Academy of Gastronomy and President of Master Chefs. To date Jean Conil has written over 100 books on all aspects of food and cookery including Haute Cuisine, Tour de France Gastronomique and Cuisine Végétarienne Française. He is consultant to Multinational Food Industries and to Cauldron Foods, Bristol.

Christopher Conil is a graduate of the National School of Bakery and a Master Baker whose ovens are to be found in Southend, England.

ACKNOWLEDGEMENT

The author is grateful to Mr Peter Fagan for his technical advice and help in the preparation of this book, and to Cauldron Foods for supplying tofu products used in testing all the recipes.

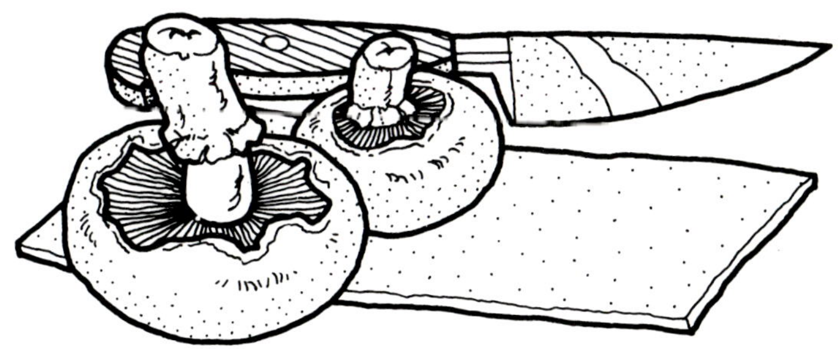

INTRODUCTION

Tofu is the original name for soya bean curd or 'fromage de soya' as it is known in French. For many years we have been involved in the development of soya bean products in every shape or form, and have seen their growing popularity. None more so than tofu!

Tofu is made by the coagulation of soya protein with an acid or other setting agent – such as calcium and magnesium sulphate (found as one of the minerals in sea water). Tofu is as versatile and useful as eggs in cookery and is even more nutritious since tofu contains no cholesterol. It has the magical properties of absorbing almost any flavour or colour and so can be introduced in a wide range of dishes.

Tofu has been the main source of protein in Asiatic countries for over four thousand years. It is only now that we in the West are coming to understand its' potential and are experimenting with it in many exciting ways. Indeed, the fact that it is a cheap food, low in fat and calories makes tofu one of the most important 'health' foods of recent times and one that looks set to find its way to a much wider public. We are completely convinced that tofu *will* assume a major role in modern cookery and that it will gradually upstage eggs and other animal proteins in our everyday diet.

There is no limit to the numerous combinations in which tofu can be blended – the recipes in this book are only a sample of its uses. Tofu can be texturised to purée with the addition of a little water and sunflower oil to give it a creamy consistency. Or the solid form of tofu can be cut into cubes or strips and incorporated in many delicious dishes, as we shall see.

There are many ways to flavour tofu, the best being to marinade in a barbecue sauce with a base of garlic, ginger, onion and soya sauce. Tofu marries well with onion and celery and is ideal in many potato dishes which are normally cooked with dairy cream and milk.

On the nutrition side, tofu is very good for everyone from babies to the elderly because it is a wholesome and complete protein which can easily be digested. For example, a purée of carrots and leeks with tofu can be given to babies and those suffering from illness. It can also be blended with cereals such as oats to give a tasty porridge.

And best of all tofu requires no lengthy cooking process. A simple stir-fry or simmering process – just to heat or crispen the dish – is often enough.

THE SOYA BEAN

The soya bean is one of the most nutritious légumes known. It grows best in hot and humid countries but in recent years some gardeners have succeeded in growing it in Sweden and Britain. We even know of some people who grow it in their suburban London gardens!

Soya beansprouts are now very popular in all good restaurants as a salad item which, with a good tofu dressing, can be a most refreshing and nourishing dish. This is because the sprouts are, when very fresh, rich in vitamin C. Soya products are used in many ways – soya flour is a favourite ingredient of the flour and confectionery industries, and is used in almond paste in cakes and biscuits. One of the most successful barbecue sauces – Lea & Perrins – is manufactured with soya, vinegar and spices and is popular in both the USA and Britain.

Soya sauce is made by fermenting the beans. Stock cubes are also made from the texturised proteins of soya beans. Tofu is also available in fermented form as Tempeh, similar to many fermented cheeses of the Brie and Camembert types. Tempeh is available in Oriental and health food shops.

The average protein content of tofu is 12 per cent. The body absorbs about 8 per cent of the tofu eaten in combination with cereals enabling a greater percentage of protein to be utilised. Hence the great reputation tofu and soya have enjoyed since ancient times. In fact the Chinese Emperor Sheng Nung in 2838 BC made the soya plant one of the five holy cultivated sources of food grown in his celestial empire, indicating just how much the ancients knew of the value of the soya bean! And without the soya bean the Asiatic and Oriental peoples would have suffered even more from the devastating famines that have occurred frequently in their history. Indeed it seems likely that soya and its products such as tofu and soya milk could be of enormous benefit in relieving hunger in the recently stricken areas of Ethiopia and Sudan, and to ensuring a steady supply of high protein food in the future.

To those who have never eaten tofu or soya products in general we have this message. Tofu should be used simply as a vegetable product and not thought of as a substitute for meat. Tofu is a basic food in its own right. We would advise all cooks to experiment with it in the kitchen, for example to replace dairy creams which contain a high level of fat. With liquidised tofu and the richer examples of soya milk available in many shops now, we are certain tofu will revolutionise our eating habits. It is one of the most useful ingredients in modern cuisine. So make good use of it!

Master Chef
Jean Conil
and
Master Baker
Christopher Conil
London 1986

1. TOFU AND SOYA

During the last war, many people survived on a very low protein diet. Although the average protein requirement is between 60 and 75g per day, we can manage with half this amount providing we eat plenty of fresh vegetables and fruits. A vegetarian diet can be complemented with tofu and soya milk in combination with cereals and nuts to ensure a good protein intake. Tofu is produced from soya milk and both should be used in a varied diet for the best of health.

If you grow your own soya beans you can make your own milk fresh every day. Many vegetarians have adopted this procedure and enjoy very good health as a result. It is better to drink soya milk than dairy milk because of its low fat content, its high protein and the fact that it is free from cholesterol. Exquisite drinks can be made with soya milk and various fruit juices, berries, herbs and nuts; from ambrosial concoctions with raspberries to a tropical coconut and pineapple mixture which can be carbonated with soda water, the range is unlimited. (It is a good idea to liquidise the fruit with some of the pulp to add fibre to your diet.)

Naturally, in making soya milk the pulp of the ground soya beans retains a good proportion of nutrients. The pulp need not be wasted as it can be used in soups and in potato and root purées.

Soya milk has the same protein content as goat milk but without fat or lactose. Most manufacturers have supplemented the soya milk with 6.7 per cent polyunsaturated fat and 19-25 per cent monosaturated. For each 100ml the soya milk has

0.63 mg riboflavin, 3.2 mcg vitamin B_{12} and 1.5 mcg vitamin D_2, and for 100ml of soya milk the total energy is 430 Kilocalories.

The listed ingredients of a 500ml/1 pint manufactured concentrated soya milk would have the following ingredients: water, soya protein isolate, sunflower oil, raw sugar, calcium phosphate, sea salt, emulsifier, stabiliser, carrageen extract and the vitamins already named above.

In making your own soya milk you may wish to enrich it with the same nutrients. However, some cooks omit the sugar and use honey. The following recipes are designed for all tastes. We have also given a list of drinks with fruits and the basic soya milk and soya flour as an alternative.

There is as much nourishment in liquid food as in solids when protein, vitamins and some minerals have been combined in the right proportion. The American habit of using the pulp of fruits and vegetables to provide fibre should be adopted by everyone. These beverages should not be gulped but sipped more slowly and the fibre chewed well. The same applies to creamed vegetable soups enriched with tofu.

Compared to cows' milk, soya milk has the same level of calcium and no cholesterol. Whereas cows' milk can have as much as 4-5 per cent saturated animal fat, the soya milk has none except in the amount of unsaturated oil you care to add. Remember that unsaturated oil contains vitamin D which is very important for the prevention of bone disease. Palm oil and sunflower oil are good sources. Alternatively, a little wheatgerm with your porridge oats and soya milk will be of enormous benefit in keeping you healthy.

HOME MADE SOYA MILK

(Makes 2.5 litres/4½ pints)

You need a heavy-bottomed pan with a capacity of 4.5 litres/1 gallon to avoid overspilling when the milk is boiling. Never fill the pan more than half full while preparing the milk at the earliest stage.

Ingredients	**Metric**	**Imperial**	**American**
Large soya beans, dried	225g	8 oz	2 cups
Water	2.5 litres	4½ pints	12 cups

1. Wash the beans 3 times in water and rinse each time. Place the beans in a colander and place under the tap for 10 minutes to ensure they are clean. Finally place the drained beans in a large bowl and cover with 3½ times their volume of fresh water. Soak overnight for 12 hours.

2. Test the beans by splitting one. If it is flat and of even colour it is ready to be used. If it is concave and brownish the beans should be soaked for a further hour in fresh water.

3. When beans are ready discard the water. The beans usually absorb twice their weight in water so weigh the beans after soaking and when well drained. Rinse once more and drain.

4. Divide the beans in half. Take 1 cup of beans to 2 cups of boiling water and fill a blender. Liquidise to a purée. Repeat until all the beans are ground and puréed. Strain the purée over a colander lined with a muslin cloth. Add 500ml/1 pint of boiling water. (This helps to extract the maximum nutrients from the purée.)

5 You should now have approximately 2.5 litres/4½ pints of soya stock. Place the liquid in the heavy pan and bring it to the boil gently. As it tends to rise on boiling it is advisable to watch the process all the time and keep a wooden spoon handy. Simmer for 15 minutes. Cool the milk by placing it in a metal container which is immersed in the sink half-filled with ice-cube water.

6 The soya milk can now be bottled and corked and stored for a week in the refridgerator. It is very bland at this stage with no salt or sweetener added. Seasoning can be added according to taste. A maximum of ½ teaspoon of salt per litre (¼)teaspoon per pint) should be added, 1 teaspoon of honey and 1 tablespoon of soya oil or sunflower oil will make up the vitamin level. For a cold drink you can blend the soya milk in a cocktail shaker; for a hot drink just heat it up to boiling point. A 15g (½oz) carob bar will give it a chocolate flavour. Many other combinations can be devised with a little imagination. Use your home made soya milk in the recipes that follow.

HONEY FLAVOURED SOYA MILK

Ingredients	**Metric**	**Imperial**	**American**
Sea salt	½ tsp	½ tsp	½ tsp
Sunflower oil	25ml	1 fl oz	1½ tbsp
Clear medium honey	1½ tbsp	1½ tbsp	1½ tbsp
Soya milk	500ml	1 pint	2½ cups

1 Dissolve the salt in 2 tablespoons of boiling water. Blend the oil and the honey. Boil for 1 minute and add to the soya milk.

2 Place all ingredients in the liquidiser and emulsify for 1 minute. This will homogenise the oil and give the milk a creamy flavour.

SOYA MILK

Ingredients	Metric	Imperial	American
Soya milk	500ml	1 pint	2½ cups
Sunflower oil	15ml	½ fl oz	1 tbsp
Glucose or honey	50g	2 oz	¼ cup
Sea salt	¼ tsp	¼ tsp	¼ tsp

1. Liquidise all ingredients. Strain through a muslin strainer. Serve with ice cubes.

RASPBERRY AMBROSIA

Ingredients	Metric	Imperial	American
Soya milk	500ml	1 pint	2½ cups
Raspberries (fresh, canned or frozen)	100g	4 oz	1 cup
Sunflower oil	15ml	½ fl oz	1 tbsp
Juice of ½ lemon			
Sea salt	¼ tsp	¼ tsp	¼ tsp

1. Liquidise all ingredients to a purée. Strain through a sieve. Serve with ice cubes and a slice of orange or lemon.

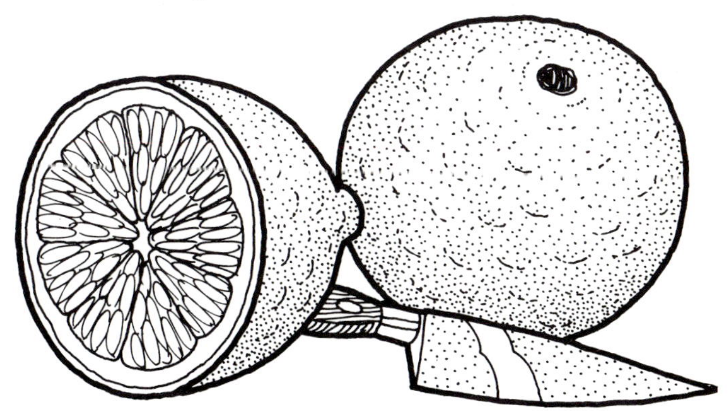

MANGO BANGO DRINK

Ingredients	**Metric**	**Imperial**	**American**
Soya milk	500ml	1 pint	2½ cups
Pulp of 1 ripe mango			
Honey	50g	2 oz	¼ cup
Juice of 1 lime			
Sea salt	¼ tsp	¼ tsp	¼ tsp
Sunflower oil	15ml	½ fl oz	1 tbsp

1. Liquidise the ingredients and serve unstrained with ice cubes and mint leaves.

TOASTED ALMOND NECTAR

Ingredients	Metric	Imperial	American
Soya milk	500ml	1 pint	2 ½ cups
Almonds, lightly toasted and flaked	50g	2 oz	½ cup
Honey	50g	2 oz	¼ cup
Pineapple juice with some pulp	25ml	1 fl oz	2 tbsp
Sea salt	¼ tsp	¼ tsp	¼ tsp

1. Liquidise all the ingredients together for 2 minutes. Strain through muslin cloth. Serve icy cold.

SOYA EGG NOG

A pick-me-up for the winter!

Ingredients	Metric	Imperial	American
Soya milk	500ml	1 pint	2½ cups
Honey	50g	2 oz	¼ cup
Eggs	2	2	2
Sunflower oil	15ml	½fl oz	1 tbsp
Sea salt	Pinch	Pinch	Pinch
Grated nutmeg	Pinch	Pinch	Pinch
Rind and juice of ¼ lemon			
Ceylon tea, brewed	1 cup	1 cup	1 cup

1. Place all the ingredients except the brewed tea in a blender and liquidise for 2 minutes. Stop the liquidiser and gradually add the hot tea. Liquidise for 1 minute.

2. Strain the mixture and serve it warm.

Note: The French would add 4 tablespoons of brandy per glass!

CAROB SPICY MILK

Ingredients	Metric	Imperial	American
Carob bar, grated	50g	2 oz	½ cup
Honey	50g	2 oz	¼ cup
Sunflower oil	15 ml	1 fl oz	1 tbsp
Soya milk (heated to boiling point)	500ml	1 pint	2½ cups
Sea salt	¼ tsp	¼ tsp	¼ tsp

1. Place the carob, honey and oil in a saucepan. Heat until it begins to boil. Add the soya milk and the salt and bring to the boil.

2. Flavour with a pod of fresh vanilla which has been soaked or by adding 2 drops of vanilla essence. Serve hot or chilled.

PEANUT PUSH-ME-OUT

This is a rich and nutritious liquid food.

Ingredients	Metric	Imperial	American
Soya milk	500ml	1 pint	2½ cups
Soya oil	15 ml	1 fl oz	1 tbsp
Juice and grated rind of ½ pink grapefruit			
Honey	1 tbsp	1 tbsp	1 tbsp
Sea salt	¼ tsp	¼ tsp	¼ tsp

1. Liquidise all the ingredients with 2 ice cubes. Serve strained or unstrained.

SOYA MILK SAUCES

Soya milk is an excellent substitute for any form of healthy, natural cooking if you're in a hurry. In line with the trendy vegetable sauces of the nouvelle cuisine techniques, you can modify these basic sauces at will. Flavoursome vegetables such as leeks, onions, mushrooms, celery, cauliflowers, asparagus and mixed vegetable soups of the minestrone-type can either be used with soya milk or with its protein/'cheese', dealt with later as tofu or 'fromage de soya'.

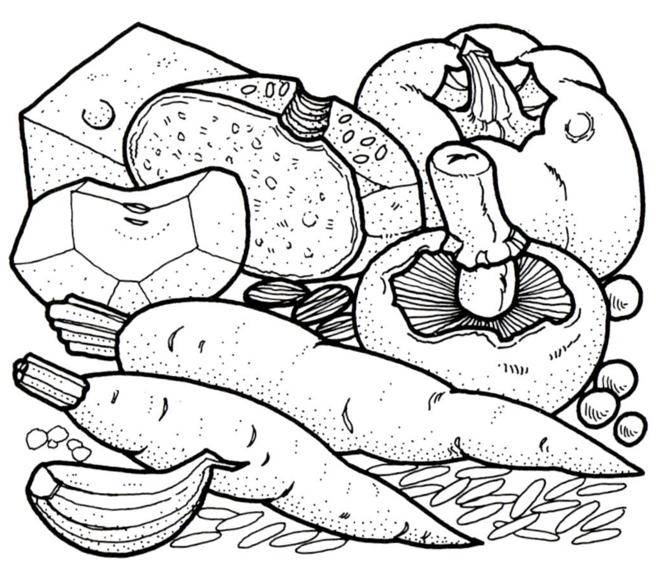

BASIC SOYA WHITE SAUCE

Ingredients	Metric	Imperial	American
Small onion with layers separated	1	1	1
Cloves	2	2	2
Soya milk	300ml	½ pint	1¼ cups
Wholemeal flour	25g	1½ oz	2 tbsp
Cornflour	1 level tsp	1 level tsp	1 level tsp
Corn or sunflower oil	1½ tbsp	1½ tbsp	1½ tbsp
Sea salt			
White pepper			

1. Cut the onion in 4 and separate the layers. In 2 of the layers stud the cloves. Simmer onion in soya milk for 10 minutes. Keep hot but away from heat.

2. Blend wholemeal flour and cornflour together. Heat oil in a saucepan of 500ml/1 pint capacity. Mix in the flour and stir gently. Cook at a low heat until you have a sandy texture without any coloration. Gradually add the strained soya milk and simmer while stirring to avoid lumps. Boil for 4 minutes and strain again. Season to taste.

   Note: More milk can be added for a thinner texture or for use as a vegetable stock.

LEEK SAUCE

Ingredients	Metric	Imperial	American
Leek, medium	1	1	1
Sunflower oil	1 tbsp	1 tbsp	1 tbsp
Basic white sauce (page 23)	350ml	12 fl oz	1½ cups

1. Remove wilted leaves from the leek. Split in 4 lengthwise and wash the inside well. Drain and slice across thinly.

2. Place the leek in a saucepan with the oil. Sweat the leek for 4 minutes without browning and add 150ml/¼ pint/⅔ cup water. Boil for 5 minutes and liquidise. Combine this leek purée with the white sauce. Adjust seasoning.

3. You may wish to retain a leek leaf which can be cut in thin strips and cooked for 2 minutes in oil. This is added to the sauce as a garnish.

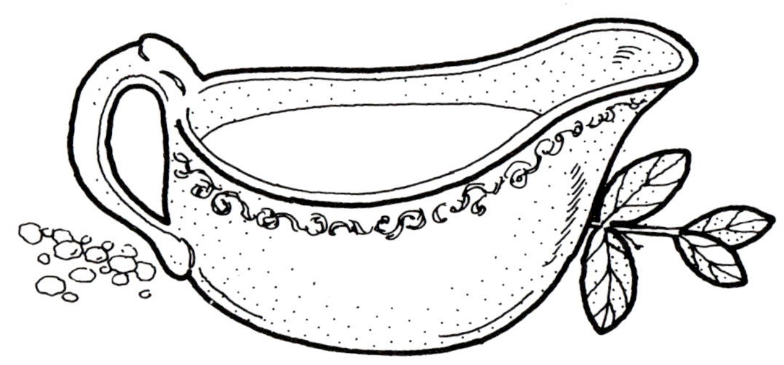

RADISH AND WATERCRESS SAUCE

This is another one of the trendy nouvelle cuisine sauces.

Ingredients	Metric	Imperial	American
Red radishes, sliced	6	6	6
Small bunch of water cress			
Mouli or white radish	1	1	1
Sunflower oil			
Peanuts, toasted	1½ tbsp	1½ tbsp	1½ tbsp
Basic soya sauce	300ml	½ pint	1¼ cups
Sea salt			
Pepper			

1. Cut the radishes into thin slices and reserve for garnish.

2. Remove all the leaves from the cress. Peel and slice the mouli/white radish.

3. Heat the oil in a 500ml/1 pint capacity saucepan and sweat the mouli/radish and watercress in it for 4 minutes without browning. Add the peanuts and 150ml/¼ pint/⅔ cup water. Boil for 5 minutes and then liquidise. Reheat this purée with the soya sauce until it boils. Check for seasoning. Add sliced radishes for garnish.

4. Serve with boiled cauliflower, turnips, potatoes or celery.

BARBECUE SAUCE

This is based on the types of bottled sauce for which Lea & Perrins is famous. It is our own personal recipe for barbecue sauce.

Ingredients	Metric	Imperial	American
Soya sauce	500ml	1 pint	2½ cups
Malt vinegar	100ml	¼ pint	⅔ cup
Dark honey	150ml	5 fl oz	⅔ cup
Tomato purée	1½ tbsp	1½ tbsp	1½ tbsp
Mixed spices	¼ tsp	¼ tsp	¼ tsp
Chilli pepper	Pinch	Pinch	Pinch
Ginger, ground	¼ tsp	¼ tsp	¼ tsp
Cloves of garlic, crushed	4	4	4

Onion, chopped	25g	1 oz	2 tbsp
Mustard seeds	¼ tsp	¼ tsp	¼ tsp

1. Blend all ingredients together in a liquidiser for 3 minutes. Leave the mixture in the refrigerator to infuse for 24 hours in a jar and cork well.

2. After this period boil the sauce for 5 minutes and then strain through a muslin cloth. Bottle and cork tightly.

Note: This is an excellent sauce in which to marinade tofu using the stir-fry method.

WALNUT AND GARLIC SAUCE

This is a sauce which can be served with leek, potato or pasta dishes.

Ingredients	Metric	Imperial	American
Walnut or sunflower oil	1½ tbsp	1½ tbsp	1½ tbsp
Onion, chopped	25g	1 oz	2 tbsp
Cloves of garlic, peeled and crushed	5	5	5
Walnut kernels, crushed	75g	3 oz	¾ cup
Basic soya sauce	300ml	½ pint	1½ cups
Juice of ½ lemon			

1. Heat the oil in a saucepan and stir-fry the onion, garlic and walnuts for 3 minutes without browning.

2. Stir in the soya sauce and simmer for 8 minutes. Liquidise the sauce and reheat to boiling point. Check seasoning and squeeze in the lemon juice.

SOYA OATS PORRIDGE

This makes a good breakfast because it is a good substantial meal which lasts you all day! And it takes only a few minutes to prepare.

Ingredients	**Metric**	**Imperial**	**American**
Water	150ml	¼ pint	⅔ cup
Porridge oats	100g	4 oz	1 cup
Soya milk	150ml	¼ pint	⅔ cup
Wheatgerm	15g	½ oz	1 tbsp
Barley flakes	15g	½ oz	1 tsp
Sea salt	Good pinch	Good pinch	Good pinch
Liquid honey, warm	1 tbsp	1 tbsp	1 tbsp
Rich soya milk	150ml	¼ pint	⅔ cup

1 Boil the water and sprinkle in the porridge oats. Boil for 2 minutes and then add soya milk, wheatgerm and flaked barley. Stir well and simmer for 3 minutes. Season with a pinch of salt.

2 Serve with honey and soya milk. We would suggest you accompany this with a glass of mixed orange and grapefruit juice for vitamin C. You will then feel sprightly for the rest of the day.

SOYA MILK ALMOND PORRIDGE

Ingredients	Metric	Imperial	American
Soya milk	300ml	½ pint	1¼ cups
Arrowroot	15g	½ oz	1 tbsp
Cold soya milk	75ml	3 fl oz	6 tbsp
Sea salt	Pinch	Pinch	Pinch
Honey	1 tbsp	1 tbsp	1 tbsp
Almonds, toasted and flaked	15g	½ oz	1 tbsp

To garnish: Compote of pears or peaches or apricots or prunes

1. Bring the soya milk to the boil. Dilute the arrowroot and cold soya milk in a cup and thicken the boiling milk with it. Cook for 4 minutes to clear the starch. Season with salt and flavour with honey and toasted almonds.

2. Serve in a soup bowl with a garnish of your favourite stewed fruits.

MUSHROOM SOYA SAUCE

Ingredients	Metric	Imperial	American
Sunflower oil	2 tbsp	2 tbsp	2 tbsp
Onion, chopped	25g	1 oz	1 tbsp
Clove garlic, chopped	1	1	1
Mushrooms, sliced or chopped	300g	10 oz	2½ cups
Basic soya sauce	300ml	½ pint	1¼ cups
Vegetable stock or water	150ml	¼ pint	⅔ cup
Sea salt			
Black or white pepper			
Fresh herbs (mint, basil and parsley)	1 tbsp	1 tbsp	1 tbsp

1 Heat the oil in a saucepan and stir-fry the onion and garlic for 3 minutes. Add the mushrooms and simmer for 3 more minutes. Stir the soya sauce into this mixture and boil for 4 minutes. At this stage the sauce can be liquidised with water or vegetable stock to obtain a thinner sauce.

2 Reheat the sauce. Season to taste and add the herbs and the lemon juice in that order.

Note: Either white or field mushrooms can be used, depending on whether you wish to have a white or brown sauce (the field mushrooms will make the sauce brown).

SOYA MILK FROM SOYA FLOUR

There is a simpler way to make soya milk but it will taste slightly different from the basic soya milk already explained.

Ingredients	Metric	Imperial	American
Water	1.25 litres	2 pints	5 cups
Soya flour	225g	8 oz	2 cups
Clear honey (not too scented)	25g	1½ oz	2 tbsp
Sea salt	Pinch	Pinch	Pinch
Juice and grated rind of ½ lemon			

1. Blend half the water gradually with the soya flour. Let it soak for 1 hour.

2. Boil the remaining water with the honey and salt and then place the liquid in a porridger to prevent scorching. Stir the soya flour and water mixture into this hot liquid and boil or simmer for 25 minutes. Strain through a muslin cloth or nylon sieve.

3. Cool completely and then flavour with the lemon juice, which will give a slightly sour-cream taste which is refreshing and very pleasant.

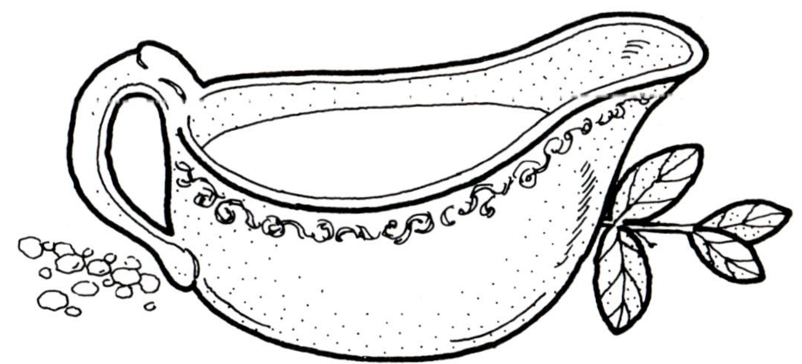

FERMENTED SOYA SAUCE

Soya sauce is made from toasted soya beans with wheat and salt. It is fermented like stout beer! The following recipe gives you an idea of the process. (You will need a 4 litre/1 gallon jar with an air lock which can be purchased at large department stores.)

Ingredients	**Metric**	**Imperial**	**American**
Soya beans	225g	8 oz	2 cups
Peanuts, toasted	50g	2 oz	½ cup
Water	2 litres	3½ pints	10 cups
Bruised wheat	225g	8 oz	2 cups
Malt syrup	150ml	¼ pint	⅔ cup
Sea salt	225g	8 oz	2 cups
Brewers yeast	5g	½ oz	1 tbsp

1. Soak the soya beans in 4 times their volume of water. Leave overnight. Drain well and bake in the oven at 220°C/425°F/Gas Mark 7 until golden brown. Add toasted peanuts. Crush the mixture with a rolling pin.

2. Blend the 2 litres/3½ pint/10 cups of water with the crushed beans and nuts and wheat and liquidise. Place the mixture in the large jar. Add the malt syrup and yeast and place the air lock on top of the jar. Keep at room temperature to ferment for 10 days.

3. Strain the mixture through a muslin cloth. Reboil it for 5 minutes with the salt. (The salt is used as a seasoning and a preservative.) Strain and bottle. Cork bottles tightly. Use as seasoning.

2. HOW TO MAKE TOFU

One of the advantages of tofu is that it is a pure protein food – free from cholesterol and extremely low in calories. In fact it has half the calories found in eggs and a quarter of the calories in the same amount of meat. And, of course, it is cheaper than meat, fish and poultry. Most important of all, tofu is a completely natural product. It is technically a cheese made from soya beans and is therefore a vegetable food. It is *not*, as some people think, a synthetic foodstuff.

The making of tofu is, in essence, the same process as extracting protein from soya beans. Firstly, you prepare a soya milk, as described earlier, and then you curdle this with an acid – as in dairy cheese-making. The remaining pulp, which is known as *okara* can be used in soups or vegetable purées. It contains protein and should not be thrown away. Incidentally, the skin of soya milk, known as *yuba*, can be used in the same way as it is equally nutritious.

It is interesting to note that the terminology of tofu and soya is from the Japanese. For instance, ground soya beans reduced to a purée is known as *go*; *okara* and *yuba* are other Japanese words also used today in the production process of tofu. Many of the recipes in this book incorporate these items as they are of great nutritional value and should not be overlooked.

TOFU (FROMAGE DE SOYA)

Ingredients	Metric	Imperial	American
Epsom salts (magnesium sulphate)	15g	½ oz	1 tbsp
Water, warm	225ml	8 fl oz	1 cup
Soya milk, as rich as possible	1 litre	1¾ pints	5 cups

1. Dissolve the Epsom salts in the water.

2. Simmer the soya milk for 7 minutes then remove from the heat. Stir in the Epsom salt solution and blend thoroughly together. Let the mixture settle for 5 minutes leaving the curd undisturbed.

3. Place a muslin cloth over a colander and place the colander on top of a bowl. Pass the mixture through to deposit the curd on the cloth. Squeeze to remove as much water as possible from the curd. Ladle the curd into shallow trays or boxes at least 5cm/2in deep. These containers should have drainage to allow all water to escape. When the curd is well drained wrap it in a polythene bag and seal tightly. It will keep for 1 week under normal refrigeration or it can be deep frozen.

   Note: Tofu should always be covered with a little fresh water otherwise it will change colour and form a dark skin, so add some water when it is finally packed into bags.

COMMERCIAL TOFU

Making tofu at home can be a tricky business. It demands a high degree of hygiene and many people, who have never made cheese or pasteurised milk, may find it easier to purchase tofu ready-made. So where can you buy tofu?

Most health food shops and many supermarkets now stock tofu in 285g/10oz packs. The better names even state the date of manufacture so that you can be sure to get the freshest and best. Tofu is also sold in softer forms like yoghurt. This can be very good for enriching soups and sauces. The medium and hard-pressed tofu is best for use as a protein ingredient with fresh vegetables. Freshness is important. Tofu should have a fine fragrance when really fresh, so check the dates on the pack.

HOW TO PREPARE AND CUT FIRM TOFU

To use solid tofu in a recipe there are a few things to remember in preparation. When unwrapping the tofu pat it dry with a kitchen cloth to remove excess water. Tofu usually is sold in slabs of approximately 10 × 15 × 2.5cm/ 4 × 5½ × 1 in. This is a good thickness for cubes. It can be cut easily with a knife to the size required. Our rough measurements may be of help to you in the recipes ahead:

Cubes: 2.5cm/1 in thick Squares: 2.5 wide × 4mm thick/1 in × ¼ in
Strips: 2.5cm wide × 4mm thick/1 in × ¼ in

To sprinkle the tofu can be chopped like any vegetable. For escalops of steaks it is best to cut the block of tofu into 8 × 5 × 1 cm/3 × 2 × ½ blocks in.

Note: As tofu is flavourless (similar to the whites of hard-boiled eggs), it must be soaked for at least 20 minutes in a soya barbecue marinade (see page 00). Any kind of Worcester sauce would also be suitable for this purpose. Tofu has an affinity for garlic, soya sauce and ginger. These ingredients can be liquidised together to form the basis of a marinade with a little oil and sherry for extra flavour.

3. SOUPS

In the formulation of these vegetarian soups, we have drawn upon ideas from many of the traditional farming communities of the world and adapted them to today's style. You will be amazed at the results! For example, in a simple slimming soup such as the Soupe de Santé with fresh lettuce leaves, you will find a rich complement of protein due to the tofu. Many of the soups included here are suitable for everyone from quite young children to the elderly. Amino acids in protein are an essential part of a healthy diet, and a good soup is the best way to ensure you are getting enough, either with tofu or with legumes such as peas, beans, lentils and cereals.

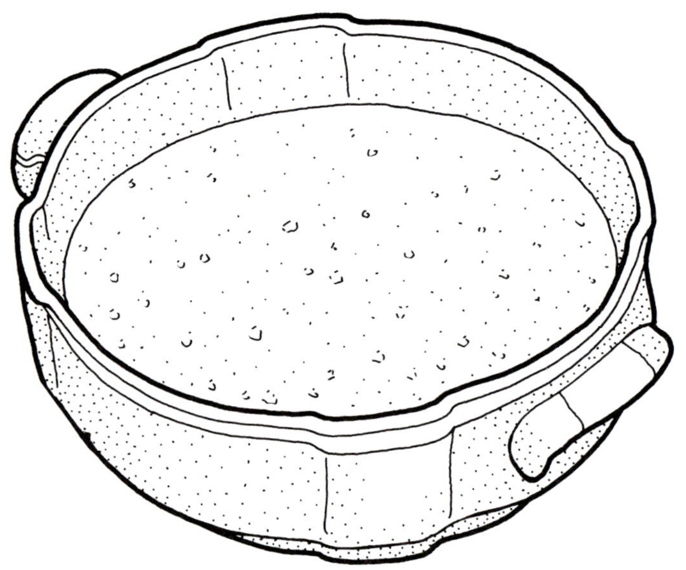

FENNEL AND SAMPHIRE SOUP

This soup is unique in that the sea flavour and acidity of the samphire highlights the dish. Samphire is known in France as salicorns and is found in sea-shore marshes.

6 portions • Preparation 10 minutes • Cooking time 20 minutes

Ingredients	**Metric**	**Imperial**	**American**
Tofu	285g	10 oz	2½ cups
Sunflower oil	50ml	2 fl oz	¼ cup
Celery seeds	15 g	½ oz	1 tbsp
Onion, chopped	100g	4 oz	1 cup
Fennel stems, sliced	4	4	4
Tomato purée	25g	1 oz	1½ tbsp
Water	1.25 litres	2 pints	4 cups
Vegetable stock cubes	2	2	2
Sea salt and black pepper to taste			
Coriander leaves, chopped	2 tbsp	2 tbsp	2 tbsp
Samphire	100g	4 oz	½ cup

1 Chop tofu into small cubes. Heat the oil in a large saucepan and stir-fry the celery seeds, onions and fennel for 4 minutes without browning. Add the tomato purée, water and stock cubes and bring to the boil. Remove head as it rises in the saucepan, and simmer for 20 minutes.

2 Season to taste. Garnish the soup with the tofu and the coriander about 3 minutes before serving. Lastly, add the samphires which only take about 30 seconds to cook.

PISTOU SOUP

The pistou mixture will provide the aroma to this delicious Mediterranean soup which we have adapted and improved nutritionally.

4-6 *portions* • *Preparation* 15 *minutes* • *Cooking time* 25 *minutes*

Ingredients	**Metric**	**Imperial**	**American**
Snap beans, yellow or green	225g	8 oz	2 cups
Courgettes	2	2	2
Water	1¼ litres	2 pints	4 cups
Thin egg vermicelli	75g	2½oz	⅓ cup
Vegetable stock cubes	2	2	2
Thin egg vermicelli	75g	2½oz	⅓ cup

Pistou Mixture:

Tomatoes	2 medium	2 medium	2 medium
or tomato purée	25g	1 oz	1 tbsp
Cloves of garlic, peeled	4	4	4
Fresh basil herbs	6	6	6
Nuts, slightly toasted	75g	3 oz	¾ cup
Tofu, chopped	285g	10 oz	2½ cups
Sunflower oil	3 tbsp	3 tbsp	3 tbsp
Sea salt and black pepper to taste			

1 Head and tail the bean pods and slice thinly. Halve the courgettes and slice thinly.

2 Bring the water to the boil and dissolve the stock cubes in it to obtain a stock liquor.

3 Wash the sliced beans and add them and the vermicelli, broken up into small pieces, to the stock. Boil for 8 minutes and the soup is then ready to be flavoured with the pistou aroma.

4 Skin, seed and chop the tomatoes if using. Their moisture is an important part of the finished dish so retain as much as possible. Liquidise tomatoes with all the other pistou ingredients to a thin purée. Blend this mixture into the soup and boil for 2 minutes.

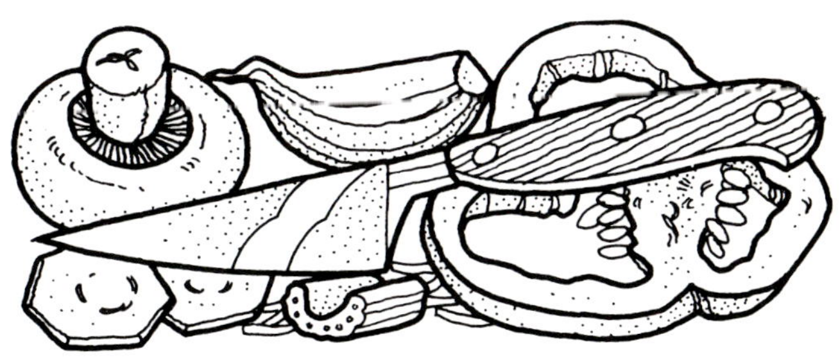

CABBAGE NOODLE SOUP

Cabbage is a very underrated vegetable, especially as a flavouring in soups! Green or white savoy cabbages are very good for use in traditional British soups. In this delightful version of Cabbage Soup we have used concentrated vegetable stock cubes or soya sauce or yeast extract, which, with the other vegetables, adds to the overall flavour. This recipe reflects a Chinese-type soup and is a sheer delight on the palate.

6-8 *portions* • *Preparation* 10 *minutes* • *Cooking time* 20 *minutes*

Ingredients	**Metric**	**Imperial**	**American**
Sunflower oil	2 tbsp	2 tbsp	2 tbsp
Spring onions, cut slantwise	8	8	8
Swede, cut into strips	100g	4 oz	1 cup
Cabbage, green	1 small	1 small	1 small
Water	1.5 litres	2½ pints	5 cups
Vegetable stock cubes or yeast extract	2 tbsp	2 tbsp	2 tbsp
Soya milk	150 ml	¼ pint	⅔ cup
Tomato purée	50 g	2 oz	¼ cup
Anis seeds	1 tsp	1 tsp	1 tsp
Small piece peeled ginger	10g	¾ oz	1 tbsp
Sesame seeds, toasted	1 tbsp	1 tbsp	1 tbsp
Honey	1 tbsp	1 tbsp	1 tbsp

To garnish

Tofu, finely chopped	285g	10 oz	2½ cups
Vermicelli or noodle, broken up	100g	4 oz	1 cup
White mushrooms, sliced	100g	4 oz	1 cup
Sprig of fresh thyme	1	1	1
Sea salt and black pepper			

1. Heat the oil in a large saucepan. Stir-fry the vegetables for 5 minutes without browning. Stir the water, stock cubes, soya milk and tomato purée into saucepan and add the anis seeds, ginger, sesame seeds and the honey. Boil for 8 minutes with the vegetables.

2. Add the tofu, vermicelli, mushrooms, thyme and seasoning to taste. Simmer for 5 minutes and serve in attractive earthenware bowls – preferably in the Oriental style!

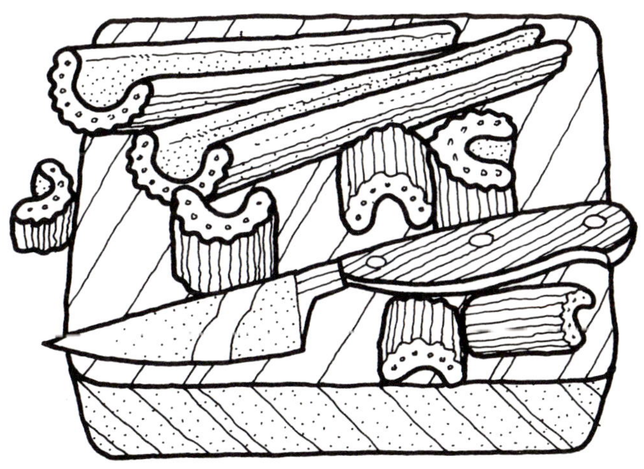

MEXICAN SOUP

This soup is characterised by the use of corn kernels and fresh green chilli to hot it up. As corn lacks a little protein the tofu more than makes up for it.

6 portions • Preparation 15 minutes • Cooking time 20 minutes

Ingredients	**Metric**	**Imperial**	**American**
Tofu	285g	10 oz	2½ cups
Tomatoes	225g	8 oz	2 cups
or tomato purée	50g	2 oz	¼ cups
Corn oil	50ml	2 fl oz	¼ cup
Sweet onion, chopped	150g	5 oz	1¼ cups

Cloves of garlic, peeled and chopped	3	3	3
Loose corn kernels, fresh or frozen	150g	5 oz	1¼ cups
Green chilli, sliced (retain the seeds)	1	1	1
Okra	150g	5 oz	1¼ cups
Water	1½ litres	2½ pints	5 cups
Sprig of rosemary or marjoram	1	1	1
Sea salt or vegetable stock cubes	2	2	2

1 Cut the tofu into small cubes. If using fresh tomatoes, skin, peel and chop them.

2 In a 2.5 litre/5 pint saucepan heat the oil and stir-fry all the ingredients except the tofu and the herb. After 5 minutes add the water and the salt or stock cubes. Boil for 20 minutes.

3 Season and add the tofu. Infuse with the herb for 2 minutes. Serve in a wooden bowl with a garnish of sliced tomatoes, avocado pears and Boston corn bread.

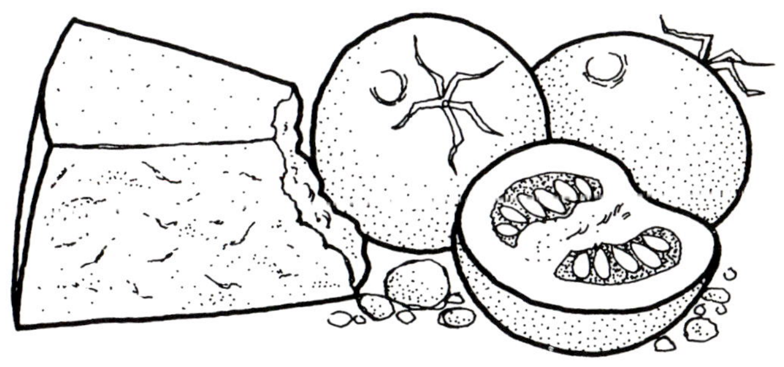

SOUPE DE SANTÉ

Lettuce and tofu soup with vermicelli!

4 portions • Preparation 10 minutes • Cooking time 15 minutes

Ingredients	Metric	Imperial	American
Lettuce	½ medium	½ medium	½ medium
Soya or sunflower oil	50ml	2 fl oz	¼ cup
Onion, cut into strips	1 medium	1 medium	1 medium
Cloves of garlic, chopped	2	2	2
Water	1.2 litres	2 pints	4 cups
Vegetable stock cube	1	1	1
Coriander leaves, chervil or parsley, chopped	1 tbsp	1 tbsp	1 tbsp
Sea salt and black pepper to taste			
Tofu, chopped	285g	10 oz	2½ cups

To garnish:

Lettuce	½ medium	½ medium	½ medium
Vermicelli, cooked	50g	2 oz	¼ cup

1. Shred the lettuce. Heat the oil in a large saucepan (1.5 litre/3 pints capacity).

2. Stir-fry the onion and garlic for 1 minute on a low heat without browning. Add half the lettuce and the water. Boil for 5 minutes and dissolve the stock cube into the mixture. Add the herbs and season to taste.

3. Blend the tofu into the mixture and simmer for 10 minutes. Place in a blender and liquidise.

4. Reheat and add a garnish of shredded lettuce leaves and cooked vermicelli. Serve.

4. STARTERS

CAULI AND CORN WITH ONION SAUCE

A combination of crunchy cauliflowers and broccoli florets with baby corn served with a soya, onion and garlic sauce might seem frivolous but what a starter to a meal for hungry people it turns out to be!

4 portions • Preparation 10 minutes • Cooking time 10 minutes

Ingredients	**Metric**	**Imperial**	**American**
Small cauliflower	1	1	1
Fresh broccoli	8 sprigs	8 sprigs	8 sprigs
Small baby corns (or canned)	8 small	8 small	8 small
Sauce:			
Sunflower oil	25ml	1 fl oz	1½ tbsp
Onion, chopped	25g	1 oz	1½ tbsp
Small piece fresh ginger	1	1	1
Clove of garlic	1	1	1
Soya milk	300ml	½ pint	1¼ cups
Thickening:			
Cornflour	1 tsp	1 tsp	1 tsp
Soya milk	4 tbsp	4 tbsp	4 tbsp
Sea salt and black pepper			
Sugar	Pinch	Pinch	Pinch
or honey	1 tsp	1 tsp	1 tsp
Parsley, fresh chopped	1 tbsp	1 tbsp	1 tbsp

1. Wash the cauliflower and broccoli in water with 1 tablespoon of vinegar per pint 500ml of water. This keeps the cauliflower firm and crunchy.

2. Boil 2 litres/3 pints of water with 1 teaspoon of sea salt and then use it to boil the vegetables for 8 minutes. Drain and keep warm whilst you make the sauce. Reheat the corn for 4 minutes and drain well.

3. To make the sauce heat the oil in a small saucepan and gently stir-fry the onion, ginger and garlic for 4 minutes without browning. Add soya milk and bring to the boil. Remove from the heat and liquidise the sauce in a blender. This is one way to avoid straining and ensure that all the ingredients are used up in the final dish. Reheat

the sauce to boiling point and thicken with the cornflour mixed with the soya milk. Boil for 4 minutes to clear the starch. Season to taste. Add sugar or honey.

4 To serve, pour a little of the sauce on to each plate and arrange in alternate rows sprigs of cauliflower, broccoli and corn. Sprinkle a little parsley over the top. Serve hot.

OKRA SOUP

The unripe fruit or pods of okra give a delicious texture to this soup. The seeds can be a good substitute for coffee.

6 portions • Preparation 15 minutes • Cooking time 35 minutes

Ingredients	Metric	Imperial	American
Red pepper	1	1	1
Green pepper	1	1	1
Sunflower oil	50ml	2 fl oz	¼ cup
Onion, chopped	1 medium	1 medium	1 medium
Okra pods, trimmed and sliced	225g	8 oz	2 cups
Clove of garlic, chopped	1	1	1
Tomatoes	4	4	4
Tomato purée	25g	1 oz	1½ tbsp
Curry powder	1 tsp	1 tsp	1 tsp
Vegetable stock cubes	2	2	2
Sprig of thyme	1	1	1
Thickening:			
Potato powder	25g	1½ tbsp	1½ tbsp
Soya milk	150ml	¼ pint	⅔ cup
To garnish:			
Rice, cooked	50g	2 oz	¼ cup
Tofu, cubed	150g	5 oz	1¼ cups
Sea salt and black pepper			

1 Split, seed and chop the peppers. Heat the oil and stir-fry the peppers, onion and okra for 4 minutes. Add the garlic and tomatoes, tomato purée and curry powder and cook for 3 minutes further.

2 Pour into a saucepan 1½ litres/ 3 pints/ 7 cups of water. Bring to the boil and add the stock cubes and the stock cubes and stir-fried ingredients. Blend in the potato powder and the soya milk. Cook this soup for 4 minutes more in order to clear the starch and to get the correct texture for the soup.

3 Add a garnish of cooked rice and tofu. Season to taste.

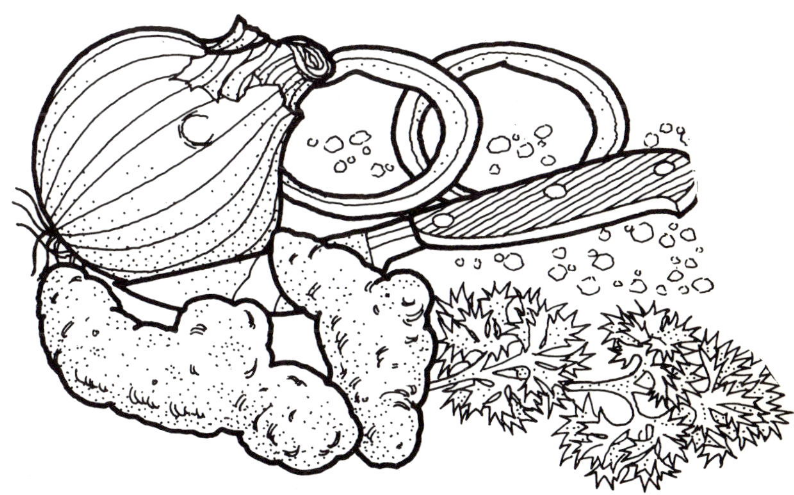

STUFFED MUSHROOMS WITH TOFU

Stuffed mushrooms are ideal as snacks. The larger field mushrooms are more tasty for this kind of dish. Make sure to use the stalks as well as the tops for the filling.

8-10 portions • Preparation 15 minutes • Cooking time 20 minutes

Ingredients	Metric	Imperial	American
Mushrooms	450g	1 lb	4 cups
Flour, seasoned with salt and pepper	75g	3 oz	¾ cup
Small onion, chopped	1	1	1
Cloves of garlic, chopped	3	3	3
Small piece of fresh ginger	1	1	1
Soya sauce	1 tbsp	1 tbsp	1 tbsp
Tofu, chopped	285g	10 oz	2½ cups
Mixed, fresh herbs (parsley, mint, basil)	1 tbsp	1 tbsp	1 tbsp
Chestnuts, cooked and chopped	50g	2 oz	½ cup
Cornflour	2 tsp	2 tsp	2 tsp
Sea salt and black pepper to taste			
Egg	1	1	1
Batter:			
Cornflour mixed with wholemeal flour	75g	3 oz	¾ cup
Sunflower oil	50ml	2 fl oz	¼ cup
Baking powder	1 tsp	1 tsp	1 tsp
Soya milk	150ml	¼ pint	⅔ cup
Seasoning to taste			

1. Remove the stalks from the mushrooms and trim the ends. Chop the stalks and blend the stalks only with the onion and garlic. Peel the ginger and liquidise it with the soya sauce. Combine all these ingredients.

2. Mix in the tofu, herbs, chestnuts, cornflour and seasoning. Add the egg to bind the mixture to a paste.

3. Coat each mushroom cap in the seasoned flour. Divide the filling into balls about the size of an egg and press on to the upturned mushroom caps where the stalks were removed. Rub each filled mushroom with wholemeal flour top and bottom. This will help the batter to stick.

4. Heat enough oil in a frying pan to immerse the mushrooms. Prepare the batter by combining the ingredients smoothly and without lumps. Dip each mushroom in the batter, drain well and deep fry in the oil. Fry a few at a time for 2 minutes. Then drain well on absorbent paper. Serve with one of the dip sauces given in this book.

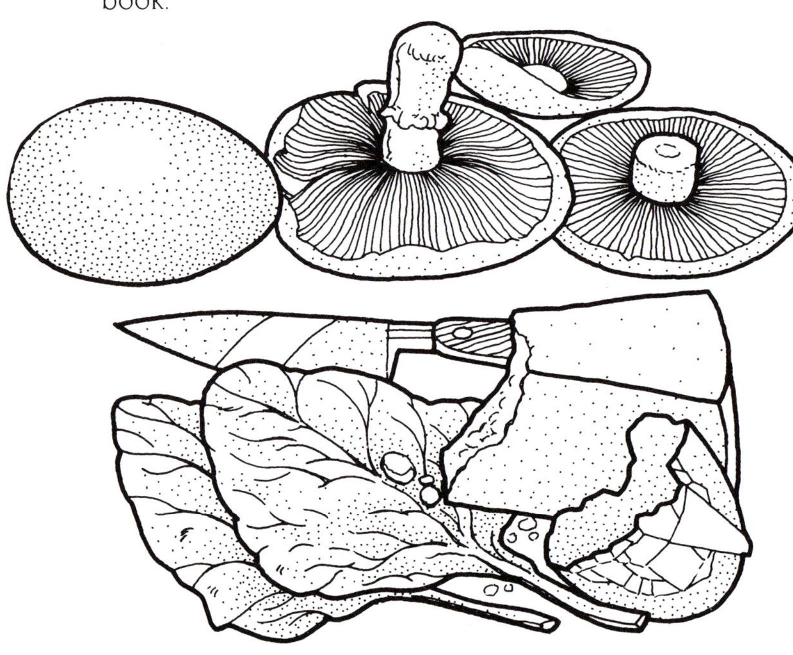

PRAIRIE WINDFALL

This is one of the most exciting of vegetable dishes and it can be prepared very quickly.

4 portions • Preparation 10 minutes • Cooking time 6 minutes

Ingredients	**Metric**	**Imperial**	**American**
Tofu	285g	10 oz	2½ cups
Red pepper	1	1	1
Sunflower oil	50ml	2 fl oz	¼ cup
Spring onions, cut slantwise	3	3	3
Celery sticks, cut slantwise	3	3	3
Mushrooms, sliced	225g	8 oz	2 cups
Sauce:			
Cornflour	1 tsp	1tsp	1 tsp
Sherry	2 tbsp	2 tbsp	2 tbsp
Water	1 tbsp	1 tbsp	1 tbsp
Tomato ketchup or tomato chutney	1 tbsp	1 tbsp	1 tbsp
Sea salt and black pepper			

1. Chop the tofu into small squares. Deseed the pepper and chop this into small squares likewise.

2. In a shallow pan heat the oil and stir-fry all the vegetables and mushrooms for 3-4 minutes.

3. In a bowl blend the sauce ingredients and mix in with the vegetables. Cook for 4 minutes stirring and tossing until the sauce has amalgamated with the solid ingredients which must remain crunchy. Season to taste. Add the tofu pieces and simmer for 2 minutes on a low heat. Serve hot.

CHESTNUT BEANSHOOT SALAD

This delicious salad contains all the elements required for a balanced meal.

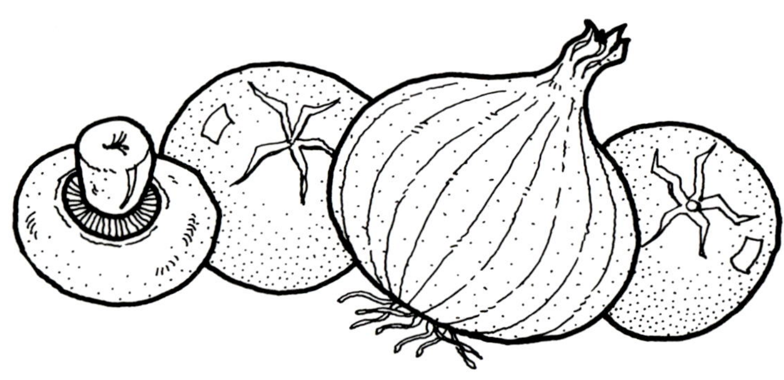

4 portions • Preparation 15 minutes • Cooking (of chestnuts) 20 minutes

Ingredients	**Metric**	**Imperial**	**American**
Chestnuts, cooked or canned	225g	8 oz	2 cups
Tofu	285g	10 oz	2½ cups
Beanshoots	225g	8 oz	2 cups
White mushrooms, sliced	75g	3 oz	¾ cup
Fresh pineapple, thinly sliced	75g	3 oz	¾ cup
Small lettuce	1	1	1
Dressing:			
Sunflower oil	50ml	2 fl oz	¼ cup
Cider vinegar	25ml	1 fl oz	2 tbsp
Made mustard	1 tsp	1 tsp	1 tsp
Pineapple juice, fresh	50ml	2 fl oz	¼ cup
Soya sauce	1 tsp	1 tsp	1 tsp
Clove of garlic	1	1	1
Soft tofu or soya milk	50ml	2 fl oz	¼ cup
Sea salt and black pepper			

In a salad bowl arrange and blend the salad ingredients over the lettuce leaves.

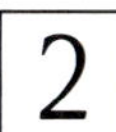
Place the salad ingredients in a blender and liquidise to form an emulsion. Toss the salad with half the dressing and serve the rest, if needed, separately. (The dressing will keep in a jar in the refrigerator.) The seasoning can be adjusted to taste.

TOKYO TOFU SALAD

2 or 4 portions • Preparation 30 minutes • Cooking time 10 minutes

Ingredients	Metric	Imperial	American
Marinade			
Garlic clove	1	1	1
Soya sauce	1 tbsp	1 tbsp	1 tbsp
Cider or sherry vinegar	1 tbsp	1 tbsp	1 tbsp
Spring onion	1	1	1
Vegetable oil	1 tbsp	1 tbsp	1 tbsp
Tofu cubes	225g	8oz	2 cups
Salad			
Small lettuce	1	1	1
Mustard and cress	Punnet	Punnet	Punnet
Lycheese, peeled	2	2	2
Stir-fried ingredients			
Sunflower oil	2 tbsp	2 tbsp	2 tbsp
Mushrooms, sliced	4	4	4
Prawns, peeled or flaked fish	150g	5oz	1½ cups
Curry powder	1 tsp	1 tsp	1 tsp
Sea salt to taste			
Cornflour	½ tsp	½ tsp	½ tsp
Water	4 tbsp	4 tbsp	4 tbsp

1. Liquidise the marinade ingredients and marinade the tofu cubes for 30 minutes.
   Arrange the salad attractively on 2 or 4 plates.

2. In a work beat the oil and stir fry all the main ingredients – the tofu, mushrooms and prawns or fish. After 2 minutes add the curry powder and cook for 20 seconds. Season and then moisten with the marinade and cornflour/water mixture.

3. With a slotted spoon take the main ingredients and place on each plate. Pour a little of the sauce over as a dressing. Serve the rest separately.

TOFU AND AUBERGINE CAVIAR

4 portions • *Preparation* 21 *minutes* • *Cooking time* 20 *minutes*

Ingredients	**Metric**	**Imperial**	**American**
Peanut oil	50ml	2 fl oz	3 tbsp
Small onion, chopped	1	1	1
Garlic cloves, peeled	2	2	2
Medium aubergine, sliced and well washed	1	1	1
Tomato paste	1 tsp	1 tsp	1 tsp
Tahini	1 tbsp	1 tbsp	1 tbsp
Seasoning to taste			
Tofu cubes	285g	10oz	2½ cups

Garnish			
Mixture carrots, clery sticks and cauliflower florets	225g	8oz	8oz

1 In a saucepan heat the oil and stir fry the onion and garlic for 2 minutes. Add the aubergines and tomato paste, and about half a cup of water. Stew this mixture together for 15 minutes and either mince or liquidise in a blender with the seasoning and tofu cubes. Check seasoning and cool when cold serve with crûdites.

N*ote*: This mixture can be spread on wholemeal brown bread but watch the calories! The tahini paste is added at the last moment when the mixture is cold it will stabilise it to a creamier texture and add extra nutritional value.

You can sprinkle toasted sesame seeds over the caviar and it can be served with or over lettuce leaves as if it was cottage cheese.

INDIAN TOFU RICE CAKES

These little cakes were served in our house to a party of children who enjoyed them more than sweet pastries! These rice cakes are perfect for teatime and are very nutritious as a main meal too.

6 portions • Preparation 15 minutes • Cooking time 45 minutes

Ingredients	**Metric**	**Imperial**	**American**
Brown rice	150g	5 oz	1¼ cups
Water	550 ml	1 pint	2½cups
Vegetable stock cube	1	1	1

Garnish:

Red and green pepper	50g	2 oz	½ cup
Seedless raisins, soaked and drained	50g	2 oz	½ cup
Small shallot, chopped	1	1	1
Turmeric	1 tsp	1 tsp	1 tsp
Cooked peas	50g	2oz	½ cup
Tofu, chopped	285g	10 oz	2½ cups
Egg whites	2	2	2
Wholemeal flour	25g	1 oz	2 tbsp
Sunflower oil	50ml	2 fl oz	¾ cup

1 Boil the rice for 30-40 minutes until it is well cooked. Drain and keep hot. Crumble the stock cube in 2 tablespoons of boiling water.

2 Deseed the peppers, cut into small cubes and cook for 1 minute.

3 In a bowl combine the rice and the diluted cube and mix well with raisins, shallot, peppers, turmeric, peas, tofu, egg whites and seasoning. Blend thoroughly. Add a little flour to bind the whole rice mixture. Cool and divide it into 16 balls. Roll in flour and flatten each one to look like a scone.

4 Grease a baking tin with a little oil and place the cakes on it. Brush their tops with oil and bake for 12-15 minutes at 220°C/425°F/ Gas Mark 7 until brown. Serve hot or cold. Children love them with ketchup or mango chutney and a crisp salad.

TOFU PURÉE

4 portions • Preparation 1 hour • Cooking time 10 minutes

Ingredients	Metric	Imperial	American
Tofu block	285g	10oz	2½ cups
Baking potatoes	2	2	2
Chives, chopped	Small bunch	Small bunch	Small bunch
Seasoning to taste	4	4	4
Chicory leaves	4	4	4
Cherry tomatoes	4	4	4

1. Cook the potatoes for 1 hour at 400°F/200°C 1 Gas Mark 7. Scoop the pulp from their centres into a bowl and pass it through a sieve.

2. Liquidise the tofu to a purée with 2 tbsp of sunflower oil, the chives and 3 tbsp of hot water. Combine the tofu paste with hot mashed purée and season to taste.

3. Arrange on 4 plates a chicory leaf. Place 2 large spoonful of the tofu purée in the centre. Decorate with cherry tomatoes and watercress leaves. Serve with matzos or celery sticks.

TOFU CUCUMBER CREAM

Ingredients	Metric	Imperial	American
Tofu cubes	285g	10oz	2½ cups
Water	300ml	1 pint	1¼ cups
Lemon juice and rind	1	1	1
Fenugreek leaves or coriander	1 tbsp	1 tbsp	1 tbsp
Garlic cloves	2	2	2
Mint leaves, fresh	2	2	2
Seasoning to taste			
Olive oil	1 tbsp	1 tbsp	1 tbsp
Cucumber	1	1	1

1. Combine all ingredients except cucumber in a blender and puree. Season and place in attractive bowls with a sprinkling of coriander or parsley. Cut half of cucumber into sticks to use as crudites, and use other half to garnish the dip.

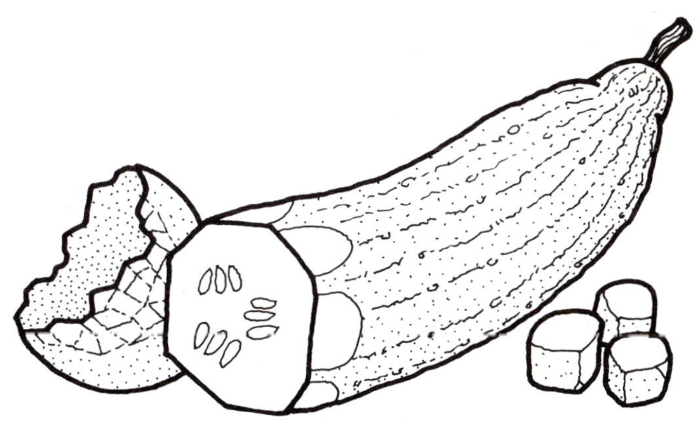

SPINACH TURNOVERS OR FRITTERS

The Greeks use fêta cheese with spinach in many dishes but it is wise to be aware that dairy cheese increases the fat content in the diet. In this recipe the cheese has been replaced wtih tofu. As an alternative to the filo pastry puff pastry can be used.

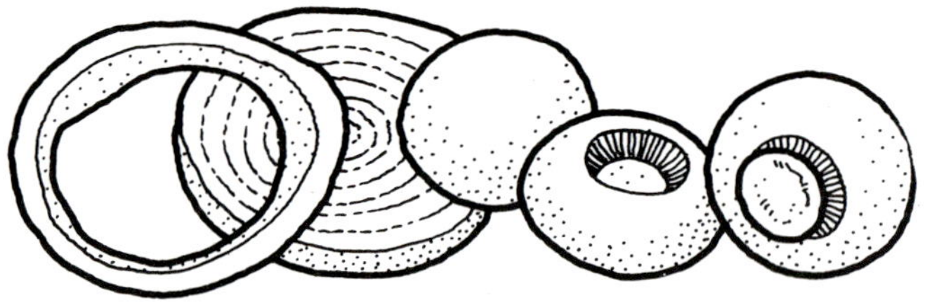

10 portions • Preparation 15 minutes • Cooking time 25 minutes

Ingredients	Metric	Imperial	American
Filo pastry:			
Wholemeal four	675g	1½ lb	6 cups
or prepared puff pastry	900g	2 lb	8 cups
Baking powder	1 tsp	1 tsp	1 tsp
Sea salt	1 tsp	1 tsp	1 tsp
Water	300ml	½ pint	1¼ pints
Sunflower oil	6 tbsp	6 tbsp	6 tbsp
Filling:			
Leaf spinach	225g	½ lb	2 cups
Tofu, chopped	285g	10 oz	2½ cups
Lemon juice and grated rind	1	1	1
Walnuts, chopped	50g	2 oz	½ cup
Clove of garlic, chopped	1	1	1
Small shallot, chopped	1	1	1
Sea salt and black pepper			
Nutmeg			

1. Combine the flour and baking powder in a bowl. There is no need to sift these two ingredients. Add the salt. Gradually incorporate water and oil to form an elastic dough. Roll into a ball and leave it to stand for 1 hour. Divide the dough into 16 balls. On a floured board roll each ball into a flat round 12cm/6in across. Brush the edges with water to make the edges stick together when you put in the filling.

2. Cook the leaf spinach, drain and press to remove water. Fresh spinach or chard leaves need only 3 minutes cooking.

3. Combine all the filling ingredients and mix well. Place about 45g/2oz of this mixture inside each circle of pastry. Fold over the pastry into a

half-moon shape. Seal the edges and crimp round with a fork to create a pretty effect. Brush the top with egg wash (2 egg yolks plus 1 tablespoon of water mixed together). Leave to stand for 30 minutes on a greased tray and then bake for 25 minutes at 220°C/425°F/GasMark 7.

4 Serve hot with a salad of your choice – lettuce, tomato, avocado, beans, etc.

Note: If you fry the turnovers the edges must be folded towards the centre like an envelope. Dip-fry 3 or 4 at a time for 3-4 minutes. Drain well. Filo pastry makes better fritters than puff pastry which is good for the turnovers.

TOFU POTATO CAKES

This is a very nourishing little snack which is very popular with children.

16 *portions* • *Preparation* 10 *minutes* • *Cooking time* 10 *minutes*

Ingredients	**Metric**	**Imperial**	**American**
Tofu, finely chopped	125 g	5 oz	1¼ cups
Potato, grated	125g	5 oz	1¼ cups
Soya milk or water	125ml	¼ pint	⅔ cup
Soya oil	2 tbsp	2 tbsp	2 tbsp
Sea salt	½ tsp	½ tsp	½ tsp
Small onion, chopped	1	1	1
Honey	¾ tsp	¾ tsp	¾ tsp
Baking powder	½ tsp	½ tsp	½ tsp
Wholemeal flour	75g	3 oz	¾ cup
Oil for shallow frying			

1. Place all the ingredients except the wholemeal flour and frying oil in a blender and liquidise to a purée.

2. Blend in the wholemeal flour to obtain a thick batter. Leave to stand for 15 minutes.

3. Heat the oil in a large shallow pan and drop in 4 tablespoons of batter to form 4 potato cakes. Cook for 1 minute on each side or until golden and cooked through.Repeat with the rest of the batter. Drain the cakes on absorbent paper and serve with salads.

CONFUCIUS' TREAT

The Great Confucius said: 'Let man eat but little and good'. These delicious pancakes are a treat for sages and mortals alike!

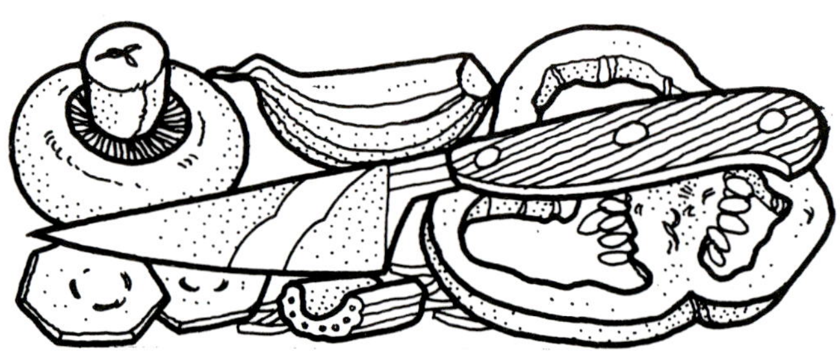

8 pancakes • Preparation 10 minutes • Cooking time 10 minutes

Ingredients	**Metric**	**Imperial**	**American**
Cooked chestnuts (crumbled)	50g	2 oz	½ cup
Pea pods (blanched for 30 seconds and sliced)	50g	2 oz	½ cup
Raw mushrooms, sliced	50g	2 oz	½ cup
Spring onions	50g	2 oz	½ cup
Beanshoots	50g	2 oz	½ cup
Batter:			
Wholemeal flour	150g	5 oz	1¼ cups
Tofu, chopped	100g	4 oz	1 cup
Water	300ml	½ pint	1¼ cups
Baking powder	1 tsp	1 tsp	1 tsp
Anis seeds (optional)	1 tsp	1 tsp	1 tsp
Sunflower oil	25ml	1 fl oz	2 tbsp
Egg whites	2	2	2
or whole egg	1	1	1
Seasoning			
Extra oil for cooking pancakes			
Sauce:			
Sunflower oil	1 tbsp	1 tbsp	1 tbsp
Small onion, chopped	1	1	1
Mushrooms, chopped	100g	4 oz	1 cup
Soya sauce	1 tbsp	1 tbsp	1 tbsp
Sweet sherry	2 tbsp	2 tbsp	2 tbsp
Sea salt and black pepper to taste			
Cornflour	1 tsp	1 tsp	1 tsp
Water	3 tbsp	3 tbsp	3 tbsp
Apple cider vinegar	1 tsp	1 tsp	1 tsp
Honey	1 tsp	1 tsp	1 tsp
Garnish:			
Spring onions	8	8	8

1. Combine the first batch of ingredients and mix well. The whole mixture can be chopped to ensure the constituents are of uniform size.

2. In another bowl combine the batter ingredients and liquidise them to a thickish batter. Add the egg whites or egg to lighten it. Season to taste. Blend the chopped vegetables, etc. into the batter.

3. Heat oil in a pan (18 cm/8in across). Spoon in 50ml/2fl oz of batter mixture at a time and cook the pancakes one by one. Cook on both sides.

4. Prepare the sauce. Heat the oil in a saucepan and stir-fry the onion and mushrooms for 4 minutes. Stir in the soya sauce and sherry and boil for 4 minutes.To make a sauce thicker, add the cornflour to the 3 tablespoons of water to form a paste. This can be added to the sauce. Cook for 4 minutes more to clear the starch. Season to taste. Add vinegar and honey last of all.

5. To serve place 2 folded pancakes on each plate. Garnish with 1 spring onion. (Spring onions can be made to curl up by cutting each end into a fringe, leaving the centre untouched.) Sauce can be served in a bowl with a ladle.

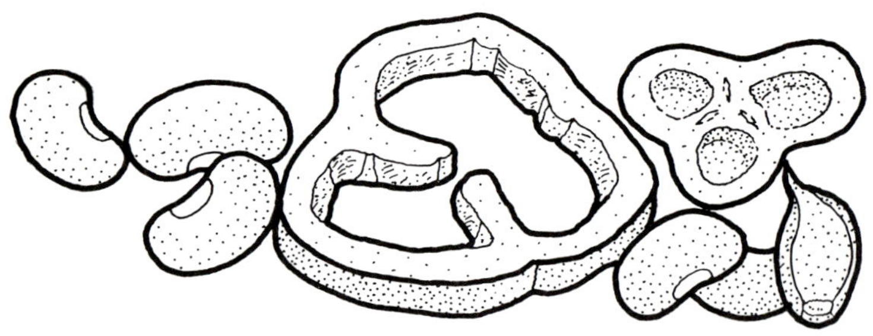

5. MAIN DISHES

To our way of thinking any meal should be nutritionally balanced. At least 50g/2oz of protein is found in 285g/10oz of tofu, and this can be supplemented by a garnish rich in vitamins and minerals. 'Energy' foods are rice, root and tuber vegetables and this carbohydrate helps to absorb the protein. The main dishes presented here are good examples of a well-balanced meal.

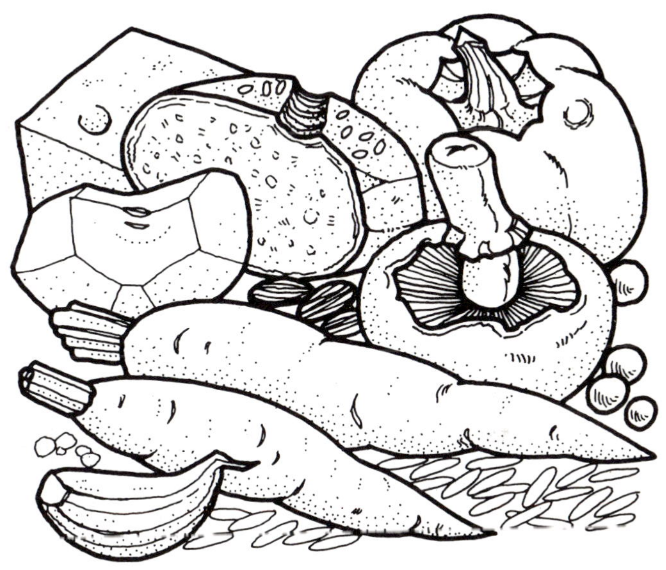

TOFU BEAN FIESTA

4 Portions • Preparation 10 minutes • Cooking time 15 minutes

Ingredients	**Metric**	**Imperial**	**American**
Marinade:			
Cloves of garlic	4	4	4
Preserved ginger plus	10g	½ oz	1 tbsp
syrup	2 tbsp	2 tbsp	2 tbsp
Soya sauce	2 tbsp	2 tbsp	2 tbsp
Juice of an orange	1	1	1
Made mustard	1 tsp	1 tsp	1 tsp
Tomato ketchup	1 tbsp	1 tbsp	1 tbsp
Green chilli, sliced	1	1	1
Sesame seeds, toasted	50g	2 oz	¼ cup

Tofu, chopped into small squares	570g	1 lb 4 oz	5 cups
Cooking oil (for frying)	50ml	2 fl oz	¼ cup

To garnish:

French beans, head and tailed	225g	8 oz	2 cups
Lettuce leaves			
Boiling water	300ml	11 fl oz	1½ cups
Red or black beans, cooked	50g	2 oz	½ cup
Rice vermicelli	225g	8 oz	2 cups

1. Liquidise the marinade ingredients. Use this to flavour the tofu by placing the tofu squares on to a shallow dish and pouring on the marinade. Leave to soak for 30 minutes.

2. Cook the French beans in boiling salted water for 7 minutes. Cool and drain well.

3. Arrange a few lettuce leaves on 4 plates and arrange a few red or black beans around the edges.

4. Heat a little oil and shallow fry the tofu squares for 2 minutes until crisp. Drain well. Boil the marinade with the oil and season if necessary. (This will be used as a dressing served separately.)

5. Heat some more oil in a frying pan and stir fry the vermicelli for 2 minutes. Place a little of the vermicelli on each plate. Top with the fried tofu and serve immediately.

TIMBALE FLORENTINE

6 portions • Preparation 15 minutes • Cooking time 15-20 minutes

Ingredients	**Metric**	**Imperial**	**American**
Spinach, cooked	150g	5 oz	1¼ cups
Tofu, chopped	285g	10 oz	2½ cups
Onion, chopped	25g	1 oz	1½ tbsp
Wholemeal breadcrumbs	2 tsp	2 tsp	2 tsp
Eggs, beaten	2	2	2
Sea salt and black pepper			
Nutmeg, grated	Good pinch	Good pinch	Good pinch
Sunflower oil			
Sesame seeds, toasted			
Coulis Sauce:			
Sunflower oil	25ml	1 fl oz	1½ tbsp
Small red pepper	1	1	1
Small onion, chopped	1	1	1
Cloves of garlic, chopped	2	2	2
Tomato purée	50g	2 oz	½ cup
Vegetable stock	150 ml	¼ pint	⅔ cup
Cornflour	2 tsp	2 tsp	2 tsp
Water	4 tbsp	4 tbsp	4 tbsp
Sea salt and black pepper			

1 Drain the spinach and chop coarsely. In a pastry bowl combine the tofu, spinach, onion and breadcrumbs and mix with eggs. Season to taste with salt, pepper and nutmeg. Grease 6 pudding moulds (approx 150 ml/¼ pint capacity) with oil and place them in the freezer to harden the oil. When this is done sprinkle the inside of each mould with toasted sesame seeds.

2 Fill the greased pudding moulds with the mixture. Place the moulds in a tray half filled with water hot and bake at 200°C/400°F/Gas Mark 6 for 15-20 minutes during which time the mixture will puff up like a soufflé.

3 Meanwhile, prepare the sauce. Split, seed and chop the pepper. Heat the oil and stir-fry the pepper, onion and garlic for 5 minutes. Stir in the tomato purée and vegetable stock and boil for 5 minutes.

4 In a cup mix the cornflour and water (as a sauce thickener) and add this to the boiling sauce. Boil for a further 4 minutes to clear the starch and produce a glossy sauce. Lastly add the honey to mellow the sauce, which should be a bright red by this time. Season.

5 Serve a little pepper sauce with each of the unmoulded puddings. You may wish to add some raw spinach as a garnish.

TIMBALE DE LÉGUMES MARSEILLAISE

A wholefood diet is now accepted as a better way to consume more essential fibre. In combination with other vegetables this rice dish will be ideal as a main course.

4 portions • Preparation 10 minutes • Cooking 25 minutes

Ingredients	**Metric**	**Imperial**	**American**
Swede, or bamboo shoots, or turnips	225g	8 oz	2 cups
Carrot	225g	8 oz	2 cups
Potatoes	225g	8 oz	2 cups
Courgettes	225g	8 oz	2 cups
Preserved ginger	10g	½ oz	1 tbsp
Tofu	285g	10 oz	2½ cups
Sauce:			
Sunflower or soya oil	50ml	2 fl oz	¼ cup
Onion, chopped	75g	3 oz	¾ cup
Garlic, chopped	5g	¼ oz	1 tsp
Curry powder	15g	½ oz	1 tbsp
Tomato purée	50ml	2 fl oz	¼ cup
Saffron strands	4	4	4
Sea salt and black pepper			
Vegetable stock cube	1	1	1
Ginger syrup or honey	1 tbsp	1 tbsp	1 tbsp
Thickener:			
Cornstarch	3 tsp	3 tsp	3 tsp
Sherry or water	6 tbsp	6 tbsp	6 tbsp
To garnish:			
Beanshoots	225g	8 oz	2 cups
Pineapple rings, cut in strips	2	2	2

1. Wash all the vegetables thoroughly and then peel them. Cut the ginger into thin strips.

2. Cut the swede (or whatever you choose to use), the carrot and the potatoes into thin slices 2cm long and 5mm wide (1 in x ¼ in). Boil the vegetables for 5 minutes in 500ml/1 pint of water. Retain half this liquid for the sauce. Drain the vegetables well and keep them hot. Blanch courgettes for 10 seconds to make them crunchy.

3 Cut the tofu into squares 2cm × 5 mm/1 in × ¼ thick. Mix with the vegetables.

4 Prepare the sauce. Heat the oil in a small saucepan and stir-fry the onion and garlic for 30 seconds. Add the curry powder, tomato purée and saffron. Cook for 10 seconds, add the reserved vegetable stock and then stir and boil for 5 minutes. Season with salt and pepper. Dissolve the stock cube and add honey or ginger syrup.

5 In a small bowl mix the cornstarch and the water or sherry. Add this gradually to the boiling sauce. Continue to boil sauce for 4 minutes to clear the starch. Now add the ginger strips, and reheat the tofu and vegetables for 8 minutes until very hot.

6 Wash the beanshoots and drain carefully. Mix them with pineapple strips in separate individual salad bowls. Serve as a side dish. Decorate the main dish with crunchy courgettes.

VEGETARIAN INDONESIAN MEDLEY

This is a mild dish which can be served with rice, meat or fish or just on its own with a pineapple chutney or mango with thin pancakes.

6 portions • Preparation 20 minutes • Cooking time 10 minutes

Ingredients	**Metric**	**Imperial**	**American**
Cashew or candlenuts	5	5	5
Turmeric powder	1 tsp	1 tsp	1 tsp
Coriander, ground	1 tbsp	1 tbsp	1 tbsp
Cocunut milk	600 ml	1 pint	2½ cups
Sunflower oil	3 tbsp	3 tbsp	3 tbsp
Large onion, chopped	1	1	1
Garlic cloves, chopped	2	2	2
French beans, halved	12	12	12
Carrots, cut in strips	2	2	2
Cauliflower florets	150g	50z	½ cup
Peeled shrimps or mushrooms	50g	2oz	¼ cup
Cabbage, shredded	225g	8oz	1½ cups
Tofu squares	225g	8oz	1¼ cups
Salt	1 tsp	1 tsp	1 tsp
Soya sauce	1 tsp	1 tsp	1 tsp

1. Liquidise the nuts, spices and cocunut milk with 600ml/1 pint of water.

2. Heat the oil in a large wok and stir fry the vegetables and tofu for 4 minutes. Add the cocunut mixture and boil for 8 minutes. Check salt and soya sauce for seasoning. Serve with plain rice or boiled new potatoes. The sauce will flavour them.

RICE AND TOFU – HANOI STYLE

The Vietnamese style of cuisine has become very popular in France today and the use of tofu with rice dishes is very trendy.

6 portions • Preparation 10 minutes • Cooking time 30 minutes

Ingredients	**Metric**	**Imperial**	**American**
Celery, sliced thinly across	100g	4 oz	1 cup
Carrot, diced	100g	4 oz	1 cup
Turnip, diced	100g	4 oz	1 cup
Courgettes, thickly sliced slantwise	100g	4 oz	1 cup

Rice Pilaf:

Sunflower or soya oil	50ml	2 fl oz	¼ cup
Onion, chopped	75g	3 oz	¾ cup
Cloves of garlic	2	2	2
Brown rice	125g	4½ oz	1 cup
Vegetable stock (made with 1 cube)	350ml	¾ pint	3 cups
Saffron strands	4	4	4
Madras curry powder	2 tsp	2 tsp	2 tsp
Turmeric	1 tsp	1 tsp	1 tsp
Ground ginger	½ tsp	½ tsp	½ tsp
Sea salt and black pepper to taste			
Sherry	1 tbsp	1 tbsp	1 tbsp
Soya sauce	1 tbsp	1 tbsp	1 tbsp
Tofu, cubed	285g	10 oz	2½ cups

Garnish:

Mangetout peas	225g	8 oz	2 cups
Baby carrots	125g	4 oz	1 cup

1 Wash and peel the vegetables except the courgettes. Blanch the sliced courgettes and drain.

2 Heat the oil in a large saucepan and stir-fry the onion and garlic for 30 seconds without browning. Add the vegetable cubes and rice and simmer for 3 minutes, stirring from time to time. Pour in the vegetable stock and bring to the boil. Simmer for 25 minutes until the rice is tender.

3 Meanwhile combine the saffron, curry, seasoning and ginger with the sherry and soya sauce. Marinade the tofu in this mixture for 20 minutes. Then add this whole mixture to the rice. Cook for 5 minutes to allow the flavour to mingle. Stir well.

4 Serve the rice in individual dishes decorated with 2 pea pods and 2 sliced courgettes. The rest of the dish might be arranged in a flat dish with the baby carrots served whole. Top with a rose-shaped tomato.

CRÊPES D'AUBERGINES AU COULIS DE TOMATES

These delicious aubergine fritters remain one Mediterranean dish loved by tourists.

4 portions • Preparation 10 minutes • Cooking time 10 minutes

Ingredients	Metric	Imperial	American
Batter:			
Tofu	285g	10 oz	2½ cups
Sunflower oil	50ml	2 fl oz	¼ cup
Water	150ml	¼ pint	⅔ cup
Baking powder	5g	1 tsp	1 tsp
Wholemeal flour	100g	4 oz	½ cup
Turmeric powder	1 tsp	1 tsp	1 tsp
Parsley, chopped	1 tbsp	1 tbsp	1 tbsp
Filling:			
Aubergine, peeled and sliced	1	1	1
Wholemeal flour, seasoned	2 tbsp	2 tbsp	2 tbsp
Sunflower oil	50ml	2 fl oz	¼ cup
Onion, sliced	1	1	1
Small lettuce	1	1	1
Avocado ripe	1	1	1

In a bowl combine the batter ingredients and liquidise to a smooth purée.

Heat a little oil in a large frying pan to produce 4 pancakes. Cook each one for 2 minutes and spread on a tray lined with greasproof paper. Cool. Meanwhile prepare the filling.

3. Soak the sliced aubergines in running water to eliminate the bitter taste. Drain well and pat dry with kitchen paper. Coat in seasoned flour as for fritters.

4. Heat oil in a pan and fry the aubergine slices until tender. Drain well. Shallow fry the onion in the remaining oil and cook until soft but not brown. Fill each pancake with aubergine and onions and arrange the lettuce leaves on top with the avocado slices. Roll the stuffed pancake up as for Swiss roll. Reheat or eat cold.

NEOPOLITAN TOFU PLATTER

This colourful vegetable dish could be presented in layers of tomato, spinach and courgettes alternated with chopped tofu and tomato mixture. This recipe conforms to Nouvelle Cuisine style and is therefore tasty and nutritious!

4-6 portions • Preparation 10 minutes • Cooking time 15 minutes

Ingredients	**Metric**	**Imperial**	**American**
Tomatoes	450g	1 lb	4 cups
Red pepper	1	1	1
Cornflour	2 tsp	2 tsp	2 tsp
Water	4 tbsp	4 tbsp	4 tbsp
Sunflower oil	50ml	2 fl oz	¼ cup

Cooked spinach, well drained	450g	1 lb	4 cups
Sea salt and black pepper			
Tofu, chopped	185g	6½ oz	1½ cups
Onion	1 medium	1 medium	1 medium
To decorate:			
Courgettes, large	2	2	2
Walnuts, chopped	50g	2 oz	¼ cup
Tofu, chopped	100g	4 oz	1 cup
Sunflower oil	50ml	2 fl oz	¼ cup
Hot water	50ml	2 fl oz	¼ cup
Sea salt and black pepper			

1. Skin, seed and chop the tomatoes. Seed and chop the pepper. Mix the cornflour and water to form a thickening paste.

2. Heat half the oil in a sâuté pan and cook the leaf spinach for a few minutes. Season to taste and sprinkle in the chopped tofu. Remove from the pan and keep hot in a dish.

3. Make the tomato chutney mixture. Heat the remaining oil and stir-fry the onion for 2 minutes until soft but not brown. Add the pepper and tomatoes and cook for 5 minutes. Add the thickener. Season to taste.

4. Groove and slice the courgettes slantwise. Scald for 30 seconds. Drain well.

5. Make the walnut sauce. Place the walnuts and remaining tofu, oil and hot water in a blender and liquidise to a thick purée. Season to taste.

6. To serve place a pool of the sauce in the centre and arrange some spinach on top. All around arrange 4 sliced courgettes and lastly the tomato chutney.

SATAY TOFU INDONESIAN STYLE

You can purchase a wooden stick for this kind of kebab and deep-fry the mixture at the last moment. The attraction for this kind of dish is the Satay sauce which can be used as a typical nutty dressing for many kebabs.

4 portions • Preparation 2 hours • Cooking time 12 minutes

Ingredients	**Metric**	**Imperial**	**American**
Mint leaves	3	3	3
Medium, onion chopped	1	1	1
Cumin, anis seeds, salt, pepper and coriander	½ tsp each	½ tsp each	½ tsp each
Honey	1 tbsp	1 tbsp	1 tbsp
Lemon juice	1 tbsp	1 tbsp	1 tbsp
Desiccated cocunut	1 tbsp	1 tbsp	1 tbsp
Boiling water	4 tbsp	4 tbsp	4 tbsp
Turmeric	1 tsp	1 tsp	1 tsp
Green chilli, sliced and deseeded	1	1	1
Tofu cubes	225g	8oz	2 cups
Satay Sauce			
Large onion chopped	½	½	½
Garlic cloves, chopped	2	2	2
3 candlenuts or cashew nuts	3	3	3
Ginger, fresh	15g	½ oz	1 tsp

Tamarind paste or lemon juice	1 tbsp	1 tbsp	1 tbsp
Sunflower oil	2 tbsp	2 tbsp	2 tbsp
Honey	1 tbsp	1 tbsp	1 tbsp
Salt	1 tsp	1 tsp	1 tsp
Peanuts, crunched or minced	225g	8oz	1 cup

1. Liquidise all the marinade ingredients and soak the tofu in it for 2 hours under refrigeration. Thread the tofu on to the skewer until it is full.

2. Make the sauce by liquidising the ingredients and boiling for 5 minutes with 450ml/¼ pint water.

3. Grill the kebabs for 12 minutes or fry in deep oil for 5 minutes. Serve with salad leaves and the sauce in small bowls.

Note: You can add to the recipe by using cheese for example in the kebabs.

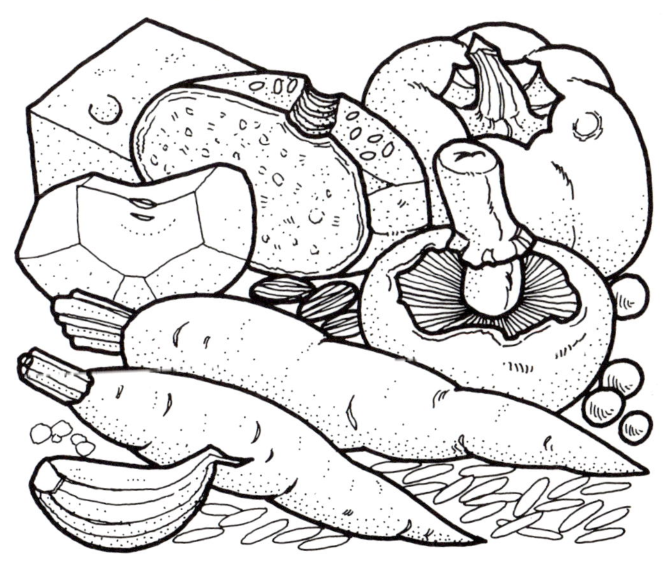

TOFU STEAK WITH ONIONS AND MUSHROOMS

A well-marinaded slice of tofu offers a new flavour and makes a perfect main course.

4 portions • Preparation 10 minutes • Cooking time 6 minutes

Ingredients	**Metric**	**Imperial**	**American**
Tofu blocks	2 × 285g	2 × 10 oz	2 × 10 ounces
Tomato purée	1 tbsp	1 tbsp	1 tbsp
Small green chilli, sliced	1	1	1

Soya sauce	2 tbsp	2 tbsp	2 tbsp
Dry sherry	4 tbsp	4 tbsp	4 tbsp
Honey	1 tbsp	1 tbsp	1 tbsp
Cloves of garlic	2	2	2
Soya oil	2 tbsp	2 tbsp	2 tbsp
Parsley, chopped	1 tbsp	1 tbsp	1 tbsp
To garnish:			
Sunflower oil	75ml	3 fl oz	6 tbsp
Onion, cut in thin rings	225g	8 oz	2 cups
Mushrooms, sliced	225g	8 oz	2 cups
Sea salt and black pepper to taste			
Bunch of watercress	1	1	1

1. Cut the tofu laterally to a thickness of 1 cm/½ in and then half across to leave 8 pieces.

2. Place all the other ingredients for the marinade in a liquidiser and purée. Arrange the tofu pieces in a shallow dish and submerge them in this sauce for 20 minutes.

3. Prepare the garnish. Heat the oil in a saucepan and quickly sâuté the onion rings until soft. Drain well and sâuté the mushrooms in the remaining oil for 2 minutes. Drain well.

4. In what is left of the oil, fry the tofu pieces for 1 minute on each side. Drain well.

5. Boil the marinade for 3 minutes to reduce it slightly.

6. Serve the steaks on a bed of watercress with the onion and mushrooms. Serve the sauce separately.

SUKIYAKI YOKOHAMA

Tofu is the national dish of the Japanese and here is one of their favourite dishes.

4 portions • Preparation 10 minutes • Cooking time 10 minutes

Ingredients	**Metric**	**Imperial**	**American**
Noodles	150g	5oz	½ cup
Leek, cut in diagonal slices	1	1	1
Tofu cubes, smoked	225g	8oz	2½ cups
Lettuce, shredded	½	½	½
Mushrooms	100g	4oz	1 cup
Sunflower oil	2 tbsp	2 tbsp	2 tbsp
Sauce			
Soya sauce	3 tbsp	3 tbsp	3 tbsp
Sake or sherry	3 tbsp	3 tbsp	3 tbsp
Water	3 tbsp	3 tbsp	3 tbsp
Stock cube	½	½	½
Garnish			
Raw eggs	3	3	3
Rice, cooked	225g	8oz	2 cups

1 Boil noodles for 4–5 minutes and drain. Liquidise the sauce ingredients.

To cook the dish place a sukiyaki pan in the centre of the dining table. (You can use a heavy based pan with a heat source of any description.) Arrange all the main ingredients neatly in separate side dishes. Have a bowl to hand to place the eggs in. Place about 2 tbsp per portion in the wok or pan. Each guest soaks a piece of the main ingredients in the beaten egg and stir fries for a few seconds, so that the food is almost raw but crunchy and flavoursome. Then the cooked food is flavoured with the sauce.

Note: A bowl of cooked rice is placed on the table for guests to help themselves.

NASI GORENG WITH TOFU

6 portions • Preparation 10 minutes • Cooking times 15 minutes

Ingredients	**Metric**	**Imperial**	**American**
Spice paste	2 tbsp	2 tbsp	2 tbsp
Mushrooms or shrimps, chopped	2 tbsp	2 tbsp	2 tbsp
Medium, onion, chopped	1	1	1
Chilli pepper	½ tsp	½ tsp	½ tsp
Colves garlic, chopped	2	2	2
Honey	1 tsp	1 tsp	1 tsp
Sunflower oil	4 tbsp	4 tbsp	4 tbsp
Eggs, beaten	2	2	2
Brown rice	375g	12oz	3 cups
Medium onion, chopped	1	1	1
Tofu cubes	225g	8oz	2 cups
Cooked peas	50g	2oz	½ cup
Red pepper	50g	2oz	½ cup
Green pepper	50g	2oz	½ cup
Garnish			
Lettuce	4	4	4
Cucumber, peeled and sliced	½	½	½

1. Make the spice paste by mixing ingredients together and liquidising with 5 tbsp of water for 2 minutes.

2. Prepare main ingredients. Heat half of the oil in a wok and stir fry the paste for 30 seconds and then remove. Clean the wok and reheat the remaining oil. Add the beaten eggs and scramble quickly. When set add the cooked rice, onion, tofu, diced peppers and peas. Season and serve with lettuce leaves and sliced cucumber.

CHARTREUSE DE POIREAUX

The flavour of leek is one of the very finest culinary fragrances!

6 portions • *Preparation* 10 *minutes* • *Cooking time* 15-20 *minutes*

Ingredients	**Metric**	**Imperial**	**American**
Leeks, large	2	2	2
Vegetable oil	50ml	2 fl oz	¼ cup
Tofu	285g	10 oz	2½ cups
Eggs, beaten	3	3	3
Sea salt, black pepper and grated nutmeg to taste			

Tomatoes	2	2	2
Cucumber slices	4	4	4
Small spring onions, blanched for 30 seconds	16	16	16
Lemon juice			
Tomato or carrot to decorate			

1 Make sure the leeks are in good condition with plenty of white and green leaves. Remove the wilted ones and split the leeks in half. Wash carefully. Cut 1 of the leeks into strips lengthwise to obtain ribbon like lengths. Boil the leeks for 5 minutes. Drain and cool quickly by refreshing in iced water until cold.

2 Line 6 ramekin dishes with the vegetable oil, and add in a green and white leaf alternating the colour. Leave an overlap which will be folded towards the centre later.

3 Place the tofu in a blender with the eggs and the other leek and liquidise to a thin purée. Season to taste. Fill each remekin with the leek mixture to the top. Fold over the leek ribbons. Place the remekins in a tray half filled with water and bake in a hot oven at 220°C/425°F/Gas Mark 7 for 20-25 minutes until set. Cover the dish with foil pierced with 2 holes to allow the steam to escape. When cooked turn each remakin on to a plate, easing it out with a palette knife.

4 To decorate arrange chopped tomato, cucumber and spring onions on the tops and a squeeze lemon juice on as well. Serve hot or cold. A rose made from tomato can be placed on top of the chartreuse or you can sprinkle a thin julienne of raw carrot on top.

TOFU CROQUETTES

2 portions • Preparations 15 minutes • Cooking time 10 minutes

Ingredients	**Metric**	**Imperial**	**American**
Tofu block	285g	10 oz	2½ cups
Carrots, grated	2 tbsp	2 tbsp	2 tbsp
Mushroom stalks	2 tbsp	2 tbsp	2 tbsp
Small onion, chopped	1	1	1
Sesame seeds, toasted	1 tsp	1 tsp	1 tsp
Celery seeds	1 tsp	1 tsp	1 tsp
Seasoning			
Vegetable oil			
Salad			
Chicory leaves, cut up	4	4	4
Spinach leaves	4	4	4
Beansprouts	3 tbsp	3 tbsp	3 tbsp
Mushroom caps	4	4	4
Peanuts	50g	2oz	½ cup
Dressing			
Low fat yoghurt	75ml	3 fl oz	¼ cup
Orange juice	1	1	1
Black pepper			

1 Mince all main ingredients and knead in a bowl for 3 minutes to obtain a manageable paste. Divide into 8 balls and flatten to produce scones. Heat oil in a wok or shallow pan and quickly fry on both sides for 4 minutes.

2 Make up the salad and place on 2 plates arranging the sliced mushroom caps and nuts on top. Liquidise the dressing ingredients and sprinkle over the salad. Place the croquettes while still hot over the salad mixture and serve. Season to taste.

WALNUT AND TOFU STIR-FRY

4–5 portions • Preparation 15 minutes • Cooking time 10 minutes

Ingredients	**Metric**	**Imperial**	**American**
Vegetable oil	1 tbsp	1 tbsp	1 tbsp
Onion, thinly sliced	1	1	1
Mixed vegetables, finely sliced or chopped	900g	2lb	3½ cups
Walnut pieces	50g	2oz	¼ cup
Tofu cubes	100g	4oz	1 cup

Sauce			
Sherry	1 tbsp	1 tbsp	1 tbsp
Clear honey	½ tsp	½ tsp	½ tsp
Vinegar	1 tbsp	1 tbsp	1 tbsp
Cornflour	1 tbsp	1 tbsp	1 tbsp
Soya sauce	1 tbsp	1 tbsp	1 tbsp
Water	3 tbsp	3 tbsp	3 tbsp

1. Brush a large frying pan or wok with the vegetable oil and heat gently but thoroughly. Add the onion and stir over medium heat for 3–4 minutes. Add all the other vegetables. Cover tightly and cook for 3–4 minutes more.

2. Add the walnuts and tofu cubes and cook for a further 2 minutes.

3. Make the sauce by mixing all the ingredients together thoroughly. Serve the dish with extra soya sauce.

STIR-FRIED TOFU AND BROCCOLI WITH PRAWNS

This is one of the most interesting of all Chinese dishes in which tofu can be used and produces a fascinating flavour.

4 portions • Preparation 15 minutes • Cooking time 10 minutes

Ingredients	**Metric**	**Imperial**	**American**
Bamboo shoots	225g	8 oz	2 cups
Broccoli florets	225g	8 oz	2 cups
Tofu	225g	8 oz	2 cups
Mediterranean prawns	425g	15 oz	4 cups

Button mushrooms, sliced	225g	8 oz	2 cups
Sunflower oil	15ml	½ oz	1 tbsp
Sea salt to taste			
Chilli pepper	Good pinch	Good pinch	Good pinch
Honey or orange marmalade	1 tsp	1 tsp	1 tsp
Cornflour	1 tsp	1 tsp	1 tsp
Soya milk	150ml	¼ pint	⅔ cup
Soya sauce	1 tsp	1 tsp	1 tsp
Fresh ginger, chopped	1 tsp	1 tsp	1 tsp

1. Cut the bamboo shoots into small strips. Cut up the broccoli florets into small pieces. Chop the tofu into small strips also. Shell the prawns and remove the cord along the tail.

2. Wash and then blanch the broccoli for 2 minutes in salted water. Drain. Wash and slice the mushrooms thinly. Heat the oil in a wok or shallow pan and stir-fry the prawns for 2 minutes. Add the bamboo strips, broccoli and mushrooms. Toss well.

3. After 2 more minutes add the tofu strips and simmer for 1 minute stirring well. Add seasoning and honey.

4. Mix together the cornflour and soya milk and add the ginger. Stir this into the main ingredients and cook for 2 minutes, tossing well.

5. Serve with a wedge of lemon.

   Note: The bamboo shoots can be replaced by turnips, swedes or white radish. The tofu can be marinaded in lemon juice with a little ginger, soya sauce and 1 tbsp of sunflower oil prior to cooking. Allow 15 minutes in the marinade to allow flavours to be absorbed.

MUSHROOM QUICHE WITH TOFU

4 portions • Preparation 15 minutes • Cooking time 10 minutes

Ingredients	**Metric**	**Imperial**	**American**
Vegetable margarine	50g	2oz	4 tbsp
Wholemeal flour, plain	100g	4oz	1 cup
Sesame seeds	2 tsp	2 tsp	2 tsp
Filling			
Vegetable oil	1 tsp	1 tsp	1 tsp
Onions, finely chopped	100g	4oz	1 cup
Garlic clove, crushed	1	1	1
Mushrooms, chopped	15g	5oz	1½ cup
Tofu, block, mashed	285g	10z	2½ cups
Black pepper			
Sea salt			

Heat oven to 200°C/400°F/Gas Mark 6. Make pastry by forking margarine into flour and then rubbing it in. Stir in sesame seeds plus enough very cold water to make a firm dough. Roll out to fit a 20cm/8in flan case, trimming edge and weighting centre with a piece of crumpled foil. Bake blind for 10 minutes.

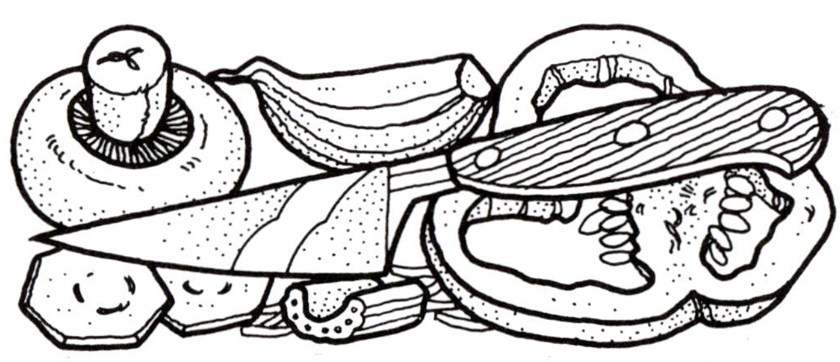

2 Meanwhile, heat the oil in a heavy-based pan, add the onions and cook for 7 minutes. Add the garlic and mushrooms and cook for a further 3 minutes. Remove mixture from heat, mix in the tofu thoroughly, adding a little water or milk if liked to make a slightly we consistency.

3 Season according to taste, then spoon into half-baked flan case and bake for 25 minutes at a reduced heat of 190°C/375°F/Gas Mark 5. Serve with a crisp salad.

NAVARIN DE LÉGUMES AU FROMAGE DE SOYA

This casserole of spring root and tuber vegetables is a very popular vegetarian dish which can be change to a purée soup in the winter and will retain its wonderful flavour.

6 portions • Preparation 15 minutes • Cooking time 30 minutes

Ingredients	Metric	Imperial	American
Sunflower oil	50ml	2 fl oz	¼ cup
Large onion, chopped	1	1	1
Cloves of garlic	4	4	4
Celery sticks	2	2	2
Curry powder	1 tsp	1 tsp	1 tsp
Water	500ml	1 pint	2½ cups
Vegetable stock cube crumbled in water	1	1	1
Tomato purée	2 tbsp	2 tbsp	2 tbsp
Turnip, peeled and sliced	1	1	1
Parsnip, peeled and sliced	1	1	1
Tofu, cubed	285g	10 oz	2½ cups
Shelled peas	100g	4 oz	1 cup
Corn kernels	100g	4 oz	1 cup
Sea salt and black pepper			
Parsley, chopped	1 tbsp	1 tbsp	1 tbsp
Mint, chopped	1 tbsp	1 tbsp	1 tbsp

1. Heat the oil in a large metal casserole dish and stir-fry the onion, garlic and celery for 2 minutes without browning. Sprinkle the curry powder in and stir. Add the water with the stock cube, tomato purée and bring to the boil.

2. After 5 minutes add the root vegetables and cook for a further 10 minutes. Finally add the tofu, shelled peas and corn kernels and cook for 4 minutes more. Season to taste. Sprinkle the hot pot of vegetables with chopped herbs just before serving.

6. SNACKS

Children should be encouraged to eat more savoury snacks rather than sweets. We have found that children love cheesy, crunchy snacks better than rather sickening cream concoctions that some mothers like to lavish on children at parties. The result is that we get sick children missing school the next day with stomach ache! Many birthday parties and other celebrations would be more successful with a healthy menu. Here are some ideas that we have found work wonders.

GNOCCHI TOFU POLENTA

Cornmeal semolina pudding is the staple diet of most central European countries and also in many African and Latin American countries, although the Roman Gnocchi is by far the best known. This innovation on our part to bring tofu into this recipes should be welcomed as corn protein does not contain the essential amino acids needed by the body.

4 portions • Preparation 10 minutes • Cooking time 15 minutes

Ingredients	**Metric**	**Imperial**	**American**
Water	300ml	½ pint	1¼ cups
Sea salt	1 tsp	1 tsp	1 tsp
Corn semolina	50g	2 oz	½ cup
Tofu, chopped	100g	4 oz	1 cup
Sunflower oil	50ml	2 fl oz	¼ cup
Black pepper to taste			
Vegetable oil for frying			

1. Boil the salted water in a pan and sprinkle in the corn semolina gently to avoid lumps. Stir well and cook for 5 minutes.

2. Liquidise the chopped tofu and sunflower oil to a paste. Blend the tofu and cornmeal paste thoroughly while still hot. Season with pepper to taste. Cool. Divide the mixture into 10 balls and shape them like scones.

3. Heat the vegetable oil in the frying pan and shallow fry the gnocchi on both sides until golden – about 1 minute. Serve hot with cold sliced tomato and lettuce leaves.

CROQUEMITAINE

4 portions • Preparation 10 minutes • Cooking time 4 minutes

Ingredients	**Metric**	**Imperial**	**American**
Filling:			
Peanuts, toasted	50g	2 oz	½ cup
Sunflower oil	50ml	2 fl oz	¼ cup
Yeast extract	25ml	1 fl oz	1½ tbsp
Tofu	285g	10 oz	2½ cups
Tomato purée or tomato chutney	1 tsp	1 tsp	1 tsp

1. Combine all ingredients in a large bowl, mix well and then liquidise to a purée.

2. Toast slices of bread and spread the mixture on thinly. Serve immediately.

CARRIBEAN SWEET POTATO CAKES

Sweet potatoes are on sale in most ethnic shops. Their sweet taste will appeal to children – and they are much healthier than a bar of chocolate!

4 portions • Preparation 15 minutes • Cooking time 25 minutes

Ingredients	**Metric**	**Imperial**	**American**
Sweet potatoes	225g	8 oz	2 cups
Tofu, chopped	285g	10 oz	2½ cups
Egg, beaten	1	1	1
Sea salt and black pepper			
Sunflower oil	50ml	2 fl oz	¼ cup

Desiccated coconut, toasted	50g	2 oz	¼ cup

1. Peel the potatoes and cut in small slices. Boil in salted water for 12 minutes until soft. Drain well and pass through a sieve to purée.

2. Add the chopped tofu, beaten egg and seasoning. Combine well to obtain a well amalgamated purée. Cool and divide the mixture into 8 balls. Shape the balls into scones by flattening them a little.

3. Place the scones on a well greased tray. Brush their tops with a little oil. Bake for 10 minutes in a very hot oven at 220°C/425°F/Gas Mark 7. Then sprinkle the coconut over them. This delicious little snack can be served cold or reheated, with a little sweet pickle or mango chutney.

TOFU NUTTY FRITTERS

Tofu is similar to ordinary cheese and has the same properties of coagulation on frying. Cheese fritters are popular at any time of day.

8 *portions* • *Preparation* 10 *minutes* • *Cooking time* 5 *minutes*

Ingredients	**Metric**	**Imperial**	**American**
Sunflower oil	50ml	2 fl oz	¼ cup
Onion, chopped	25g	1½ oz	2 tbsp
Cloves of garlic, chopped	2	2	2
Tofu, chopped	285g	10 oz	2½ cups
Yeast extract	1 tsp	1 tsp	1 tsp
Egg, beaten	1	1	1
Carrots, finely grated	2 tbsp	2 tbsp	2 tbsp
Wholemeal flour	25g	1 oz	1½ tbsp
Peanuts, toasted	50g	2 oz	¼ cup
Sesame seeds, toasted	25g	1 oz	1½ tbsp

1 Heat the oil in a shallow pan and stir-fry the onion and garlic for 2 minutes without browning. Add the tofu and yeast extract and cook for 3 minutes. Cool and place the mixture in a large bowl.

2 Blend in the egg, carrots, flour and peanuts. Divide the mixture into 8 balls. Flatten them slightly and refry them in a little oil until golden brown. Sprinkle sesame seeds on top and serve on lettuce leaves.

TARTARE TOFU DIP

4 portions • Preparation 10 minutes • Cooking time 5 minutes

Ingredients	**Metric**	**Imperial**	**American**
Sunflower oil	50ml	2 fl oz	¼ cup
Onion, chopped	50g	2 oz	½ cup
Tofu, chopped finely	285g	10 oz	2½ cups
Water, hot	50ml	2 fl oz	¼ cup
To garnish:			
Parsley and tarragon	2 tbsp	2 tbsp	2 tbsp
Small gherkins, chopped	2	2	2
Anchovy fillets, chopped	2	2	2
Made mustard	1 tsp	1 tsp	1 tsp
Lemon juice	1 tbsp	1 tbsp	1 tbsp
Honey	1 tsp	1 tsp	1 tsp

1 Heat the oil in a pan and stir-fry the onion until soft. Add the tofu and reheat for 3 minutes.

2 Purée the mixture in a blender with a little hot water. Transfer the mixture to a mixing bowl and combine all the garnishing ingredients to serve.

POTATO YAM YAM

Sweet potatoes and Jerusalem artichokes have one thing in common, they both are naturally sweet. The combination of these produces an interesting flavour worth trying, especially with the tofu enrichment which makes it a very simple and nourishing meal.

4 portions • Preparation 10 minutes • Cooking time 35 minutes

Ingredients	**Metric**	**Imperial**	**American**
Potatoes	225g	8 oz	2 cups
Jerusalem artichokes	225g	8 oz	2 cups
Soya milk	550ml	1 pint	2½ cups
Cloves of garlic, chopped	2	2	2
Tofu, sliced in small squares	285g	10 oz	2½ cups
Small onion, sliced	1	1	1
Sea salt and black pepper			
Small sprig of fresh thyme	1	1	1

1. Wash, peel and slice the potatoes and artichokes. Scald the potatoes in boiling salted water and drain immediately.

2. Liquidise the soya milk and garlic and pour over the potatoes in an deep earthenware dish. Arrange the tofu slices as a middle layer and add the artichokes and onions on top. Season to taste and place the thyme in the centre of the mixture on top.

3. Bake at 200°C/400°F/ Gas Mark 8 for 35-40 minutes. Cover with a lid to retain the fragrant flavour.

TOMATO DIP PROVENÇALE

For this dip you will need summer ribbed tomatoes, sold in Britain as steak or stuffing tomatoes. The flavour can be reinforced with tomato purée or ketchup if preferred.

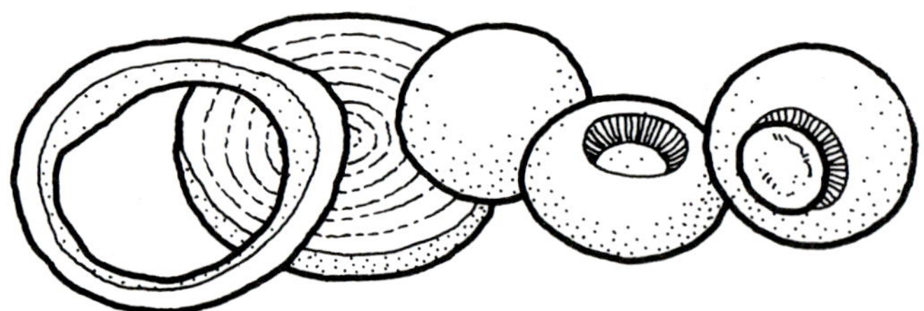

4 portions • Preparation 12 minutes • Cooking time 8 minutes

Ingredients	**Metric**	**Imperial**	**American**
Sunflower or soya oil	50ml	2 fl oz	¼ cup
Medium onion, chopped	1	1	1
Cloves of garlic, chopped	2	2	2
Large tomatoes, chopped	4	4	4
Tomato purée	50g	2 oz	3 tbsp
Thickener:			
Cornstarch	2 tsp	2 tsp	2 tsp
Red wine or water	6 tbsp	6 tbsp	6 tbsp
Tofu, chopped	285g	10 oz	2½ cups
Sea salt and black pepper to taste			
Juice of lemon	½	½	½

1 Heat the oil in a small saucepan. Stir-fry the onion and garlic for 30 seconds without browning. Add the chopped tomatoes and tomato purée and cook for 4 minutes.

2 In a small bowl blend the cornstarch with wine or water and add to the main mixture to thicken it to a marmalade-like mixture. Place the tomato mixture and tofu in a liquidiser and blend to a thick purée. Season to taste and add lemon juice.

3 Crûdités can be made from 450g/1 lb/4 cups assorted carrot, celery, cauliflower florets, raw mushrooms, courgettes, cucumber, celery, etc. All should be cut into sticks about 4 cm long × 5mm thick (2in × ¼ in). As an alternative use Ritz or rice crackers.

WATERCRESS AND LEEK TOFU DIP

This particular dish is best served with mouli or radish crûdités or piped as a filling into the hollowed out centre of a cucumber.

4 portions • Preparation 10 minutes • Cooking time 8 minutes

Ingredients	**Metric**	**Imperial**	**American**
Sunflower or sesame oil	100ml	4 fl oz	½ cup
Leeks, medium	2	2	2
Tofu, chopped	285g	10 oz	2½ cups
Mashed potatoes, hot	50g	2 oz	¼ cup
Sea salt and black pepper to taste			
Made mustard, sweet	1 tsp	1 tsp	1 tsp
Honey	1 tsp	1 tsp	1 tsp
Bunch of watercress (leaves only)	1	1	1

1. Heat the oil in a pan and stir-fry the leeks for 2 minutes. Then add water and boil for 5 minutes until soft. Blend the tofu and potatoes together and mix well with a spoon. Season to taste and remove from heat.

2. Add the mustard and honey. Purée the mixture with the watercress leaves in a blender with the remaining oil. This will make the dip creamier. Serve with crûdités as mentioned above.

MEXICAN TORTILLA

There is no reason why a cook should not take advantage of tofu and soya milk to improve a dish which has been for many centuries the very staff of life for many of the Latin American countries.

4 *portions* • *Preparation* 10 *minutes* • *Cooking time* 5 *minutes*

Ingredients	**Metric**	**Imperial**	**American**
Cornmeal	225g	8oz	2 cups
Boiling water	100ml	4 fl oz	½ cup
Wholemeal flour	225g	8 oz	2½ cups
Baking powder	25g	1 oz	2 tbsp
Soya milk, cold	125ml	4 fl oz	½ cup
Sea salt	1 tsp	1 tsp	1 tsp
Sunflower or corn oil	25ml	1 fl oz	2 tbsp

1. Place the cornmeal in a bowl and soak it with the boiling water to prevent grittiness. Add the flour mixed with the baking powder and gradually the soya milk to obtain a smooth dough. The baking powder must be blended with the flour beforehand or use self-raising flour. Sprinkle in the salt and knead the dough well. Rest it for 1 hour and then divide it into 8 balls. Sprinkle a little flour over each and roll to 4cm/2 in across.

2. Grease a griddle pan and cook the tortillas on both sides for 3-4 minutes. Brush a rolling pin with oil and place the tortillas on the rolling pin to dry as if you were hanging some linen on a line. When dried the tortillas will be crisp and curled.

3. For filling you can use baked beans mashed up with chopped tofu and refried with a little oil. Arrange a leaf of lettuce on top of the tortilla and spoon the bean mixture on.

RATATOUILLE TOFU DIP WITH AUBERGINE FRITTERS

6 portions • Preparation 12 minutes • Cooking time 20 minutes

Ingredients	**Metric**	**Imperial**	**American**
Aubergine, medium	1	1	1
Red pepper	1	1	1
Green pepper	1	1	1
Courgette	1	1	1
Small onion	1	1	1
Cloves of garlic	2	2	2
Sunflower oil	50ml	2 fl oz	¼ cup
Sea salt and black pepper			

Tofu	285g	10 oz	2½ cups
Worcester sauce	1 tbsp	1 tbsp	1 tbsp

For aubergine fritters:

Half aubergine from above list			
Wholemeal flour	50g	2 oz	½ cup
Egg or egg white	1	1	1
Porridge oats	50g	2 oz	½ cup
Sea salt and black pepper			
Sunflower oil			

1. Cut the aubergine half. One half should be cut into cubes, the other into thick slices (4mm/¼in) Reserve the slices for the garnish.

2. Split the peepers, remove the seeds and dice into cubes. Slice the courgette. Peel the onion and garlic and chop both finely.

3. Heat the oil in a large pan and shallow fry the vegetables for 5 minutes. Then cover the vegetables with water, add salt and pepper and boil for 15 minutes. Add the tofu and boil for a further 5 minutes. Drain and liquidise the vegetable mixture with the Worcester sauce to a purée.

4. Reheat the purée in a pan and thicken it with 1 tablespoon of cornflour mixed in 4 tablespoons of cold water. Cool and season the purée which should be thick. It can be served into small bowls.

5. Wash the sliced aubergine and dry with kitchen paper. Season and coat it in flour, then in the egg and then finally roll into the porridge oats.

6. Heat the oil in a pan and shallow fry the fritters for 1½ minutes on each side until golden. Drain well and season with salt and pepper. They can be served with the dip and with a sprig of parsley to garnish.

PICKLED TOFU WITH VEGETABLES

This is an unusual way of flavouring tofu and serving it as a pickle. It keeps for 1 week in the fridge.

4 portions • Preparation 10 minutes • Blanching 1 minute

Ingredients	**Metric**	**Imperial**	**American**
Large carrot	1	1	1
Medium turnip	1	1	1
Medium swede	1	1	1
Celery sticks	2	2	2
Red pepper	1	1	1
Yellow pepper	1	1	1
Green chilli peppers	2	2	2
Pickling spices - coriander, ginger, black pepper corns	1 tbsp	1 tbsp	1 tbsp
Tofu block	285g	10 oz	2½ cups
Pickling mixture:			
Cider vinegar	500ml	1 pint	2½ cups
Onion, sliced	1	1	1
Cloves of garlic	2	2	2
Honey	450g	1 lb	2 cups
Sea salt	1 tsp	1 tsp	1 tsp
Sunflower oil	50ml	2 fl oz	¼ cup
Celery seeds	2 tsp	2 tsp	2 tsp
Anis seeds	2 tsp	2 tsp	2 tsp
Water	300ml	½ pint	1¼ cups

1. Boil the pickling mixture for 5 minutes and let it cool completely.

2. Peel, wash and cut the vegetables into sticks 4cm/2 in long. Scald them in boiling salted water for 30 seconds. Refresh in cold water until cool and drain well.

3. Place the vegetables in suitable jars covered with the cold pickling mixture. Leave to marinade for 3 days under refrigeration then add the tofu cut into strips. Leave in the mixture for 2 more days in the refrigerator. Use as a pickle with hot potato or rice dishes.

TOFU SALAD DRESSING

Preparation 5 minutes

Ingredients	**Metric**	**Imperial**	**American**
Tofu	285g	10 oz	2½ cups
Sunflower or soya oil	100ml	4 fl oz	½ cup
Tahini paste	15g	½ oz	1 tbsp
Made mustard	1 tsp	1 tsp	1 tsp
Cider vinegar	1 tbsp	1 tbsp	1 tbsp
Honey	1 tsp	1 tsp	1 tsp
Sea salt and black pepper			
Turmeric powder	¼ tsp	¼ tsp	¼ tsp

1. Purée all ingredients in a blender until smooth and thickish. Adjust texture and the seasoning if required.

Note: This dressing can be modified with mango chutney, tomato sauce or mixed green herbs for a different flavour.

PEARS WITH FROMAGE DE SOYA A LA CONIL

This is one of many favourite dips Jean has served at the Arts Clubs for various functions. It can be spread on brown bread as a sandwich filling or thinned down with fruit juice to be used as a salad dressing or, as in this recipe, served as a sauce with pears.

6 portions • Preparation 10 minutes

Ingredients	Metric	Imperial	American
Tofu, chopped	285g	10 oz	2½ cups
Bunch watercress (leaves only)	1	1	1
Mint leaves, fresh	4	4	4
Cloves of garlic, peeled	4	4	4
Spring onions	4	4	4
Basil leaves, fresh	3	3	3
Lemon juice and grated rind of lemon	1	1	1
Radishes, washed and sliced	4	4	4
Made mustard, sweet	1 tsp	1 tsp	1 tsp
Sea salt and black pepper			
Soya sauce	25ml	1 fl oz	2 tbsp
Sunflower oil	25ml	1 fl oz	2 tbsp
To garnish:			
Comice pears, ripe	2	2	2
Cranberries, fresh	100g	4 oz	1 cup
Sprigs fo watercress	6	6	6

1. Wash the spring onions and slice them coarsely. Place all the ingredients in a liquidiser and blend to a thick purée. Season to taste.

2. Peel the pears and slice them lengthwise. Pour 4 tablespoons of the purée mixture on to each plate and arrange the pears in artistic style. Decorate with cranberries and watercress.

Note: The alternative use for this dressing is as a dip and served with root crûdités, Belgian endives or boiled new potatoes.

TOASTED CLUB TOFU SANDWICH

Tofu is a very good vegetarian substitute for dairy cheese and vegans will find this type of toasted sandwich very much to their taste.

4 portions • Preparation 10 minutes • Toasting 5 minutes

Ingredients	Metric	Imperial	American
Tofu block	285g	10 oz	2½ cups
Wholemeal bread slices	8	8	8
White mushrooms, sliced	225g	8 oz	2 cups
Marinade:			
Clove of garlic, chopped	1	1	1
Small onion, chopped	1	1	1
Worcester sauce	2 tbsp	2 tbsp	2 tbsp
Sunflower oil	1 tbsp	1 tbsp	1 tbsp
Parsley, chopped	1 tsp	1 tsp	1 tsp
Seasoning to taste			

1. Cut the tofu into 4 slices to fit the bread.

2. Liquidise the marinade ingredients and place the liquid into a shallow dish. Toss the mushrooms in this sauce and marinade for 10 minutes. Drain well. Marinade the tofu slices in what is left of the sauce for 10 minutes.

3. Place the tofu slices in a frying pan or baking tray and fry or grill for 3 minutes.

4. On 4 slices of toasted wholemeal bread arrange 1 slice each of tofu and sprinkle raw marinaded mushrooms on top. Add lettuce leaves and cap with the remaining slices of bread. Serve hot.

BAKED BANANA TOFU PIE

Unripe bananas are ideal for this Asiatic dish flavoured with chilli peppers and toasted peanut sauce.

4 portions • Preparation 10 minutes • Cooking time 20 minutes

Ingredients	Metric	Imperial	American
Barbecue marinade peanut sauce:			
Cider vinegar	1 tbsp	1 tbsp	1 tbsp
Small green chilli, sliced	1	1	1
Peanuts, toasted	75g	3 oz	¾ cup
Hot water	75ml	3 fl oz	6 tbsp
Worcester sauce	25ml	1½ tbsp	1 fl oz
Cloves of garlic, crushed	2	2	2
Small onion, chopped	1	1	1
Unripe bananas	4	4	4
Tofu	285g	10 oz	2½ cups

1. Liquidise all marinade ingredients. Boil the mixture for 4 minutes.

2. Peel and slice the bananas. Cut the tofu into thin strips. Place the bananas in a saucepan and boil in the marinade for 20 minutes until they are cooked. Add the tofu and reheat for 4 minutes. Serve in individual dishes with a bowl of cooked rice.

TOFU BREAD

6 portions • Preparation 10 minutes • Cooking time 8-10 minutes

Ingredients	Metric	Imperial	American
Wholemeal flour	225g	8 oz	2 cups
Baking powder	15g	½ oz	½ tbsp
Sea salt	½ tsp	½ tsp	½ tsp
Demerara sugar or honey	½ tsp	½ tsp	½ tsp
Soya milk	100ml	4 fl oz	½ cup
Sunflower oil	25ml	1 fl oz	1½ tbsp
Filling:			
Tomato beans, baked and mashed up	100g	4 oz	1 cup
Avocado, peeled and sliced	1	1	1
Lettuce leaves	4	4	4

1. In a mixing bowl combine the flour, baking powder, salt and sugar or honey. Blend well. Make into a firm dough with soya milk and oil. Knead well and divide into 8 balls, each the size of an egg.

2. Dust the pastry board with wholemeal flour and flatten each ball to an oval shape about 8 × 4 cm/3½ × 1½ in. Place the rolls on a greased tray and bake for 10 minutes at 220°/425°F/Gas Mark 7.

3. Blend the mashed beans with the diced avocado and insert a spoonful of this mixture with a lettuce leaf inside each roll.

7. DESSERTS

The less sugar or sweets you eat the better for your health it is! For children who need energy honey is the best alternative to sugar. In the same way soya milk and bean curd can replace dairy milk and cream cheese in most desserts, for example, in custards, rice puddings, blancmange, cakes and breads.

LEMON TOFU HONEY TORTE

This adaptation of a lemon cheese cake using tofu instead of dairy cheese has been well received by my vegetarian clientele. It is based on a flapjack pastry base which is crunchy and pleasant to eat.

8 portions • *Preparation* 10 *minutes* • *Cooking time* 20 *minutes*

Ingredients	**Metric**	**Imperial**	**American**
Pastry Base:			
Vegetable fat, hard	225g	8 oz	1 cup
Honey	50g	2 oz	¼ cup
Demerara sugar	50g	2 oz	¼ cup
Oats	350g	12 oz	3 cups
Cashew nuts, finely chopped	100g	4 oz	1 cup
Desiccated coconut	25g	1 oz	2 tbsp
Sesame seeds	1 tsp	1 tsp	1 tsp
Bran	2 tsp	2 tsp	2 tsp
Filling:			
Tofu, diced	285g	10 oz	2½ cups
Juice and grated rind of a lemon			
Drops of lemon essence	3	3	3
Turmeric	½ tsp	½ tsp	½ tsp
Honey	50g	2 oz	¾ cup
Sunflower oil	50ml	2 fl oz	¼ cup
Thickener:			
Cornflour	1 tsp	1 tsp	1 tsp
Egg yolks	2	2	2
Soya milk or water	3	3	3
Topping:			
Tangerine	1	1	1
Small bunch seedless grapes	1	1	1
To decorate:			
Toasted almonds	25g	1 oz	2 tbsp

1. Make the pastry first. Boil the fat, honey and sugar in a medium saucepan for 2 minutes as for a syrup. Pour the syrup into a bowl and mix in the oats, nuts, and bran seeds.

2. Grease a baking tray and a 20cm/9 in baking ring (or use a tin with a collapsible bottom). Press the pastry flapjack mixture into this baking sheet or greased mould to a thickness of ¼ in/5mm. Bake for 15 minutes at 220°F/425°C/Gas Mark 7 until brown. Cool until the base is firm like a biscuit.

3. In a saucepan place the filling ingredients and add 150ml/¼ pint of water. Boil for 2 minutes and place in a blender to reduce to a thin purée. Reheat again to boiling point. Thicken it with the cornflour, egg yolks and soya milk/water. Boil for 4 minutes further to clear the starch and produce a sort of blancmange.

4. Pour this tofu paste on to the cooked base and cool completely. When cold arrange in a circle sliced segments of tangerine and halves of grapes in alternate rows. (You can brush the fruits with hot honey to glaze the fruits.) Sprinkle almonds on top.

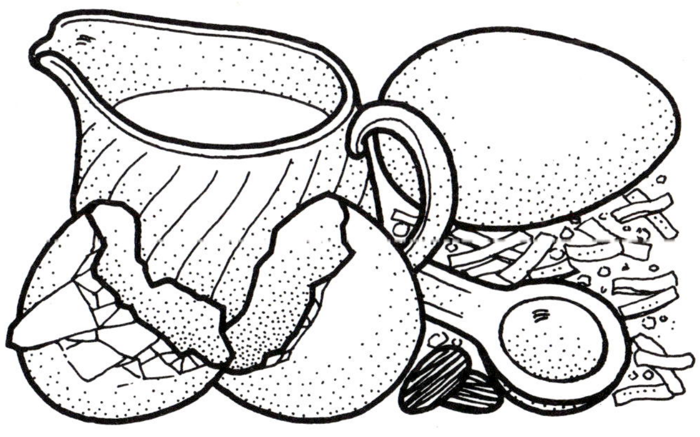

FRUIT KISSEL WITH TOFU

This is a well known Russian dessert and the tofu in this version adds protein making it a delicious sweet for growing children.

4 portions • Preparation 10 minutes • Cooking time 10 minutes

Ingredients	**Metric**	**Imperial**	**American**
Green apples	150g	5 oz	1¼ cups
Blackcurrants or other berries	75g	3 oz	⅓ cup
Honey	75g	3 oz	⅓ cup
Sunflower oil	1 tbsp	1 tbsp	1 tbsp
Water	75ml	3 fl oz	6 tbsp
Tofu, chopped	100g	4 oz	½ cup

Cinnamon, ground	Pinch	Pinch	Pinch
Sea salt	Pinch	Pinch	Pinch
Cornflour	2 tsp	2 tsp	2 tsp
Water	5 tbsp	5 tbsp	5 tbsp
Juice and grated rind of lemon or orange	1	1	1
Rich soya milk or silken tofu to serve			

1. Peel, core and slice the apples. In a saucepan boil the fruits with the honey, oil and water for 3 minutes until soft.

2. Cool and liquidise with the tofu, cinnamon and seasoning. Reheat the mixture and boil it for 2 minutes.

3. Thicken with cornflour and water. Add lemon juice. Cook for 4 minutes to clear the starch. It should be the consistency of porridge. Serve in individual bowls with soya milk or silken tofu.

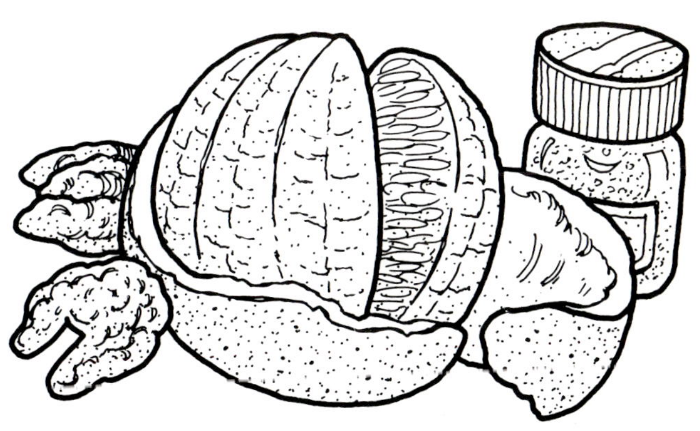

RASPBERRY TOFU SOUFFLÉ

6 portions • *Preparation* 15 *minutes* • *Cooking time* 15-20 *minutes*

Ingredients	**Metric**	**Imperial**	**American**
Soft vegetable margarine	50g	2 oz	¼ cup
Toasted almonds, chopped	25g	1 oz	2 tbsp
Caster sugar	100g	4 oz	½ cup
Raspberries	150g	5 oz	1¼ cups
Tofu, crumbled or finely chopped	150g	5 oz	1¼ cups
Egg whites	5	5	5
Sea salt	Pinch	Pinch	Pinch

1. Take 6 ramekin dishes (150ml/¼ pint) and coat the insides with soft margarine and a mixture of chopped almonds and caster sugar.

2. In a saucepan boil the raspberries and tofu for 3 minutes. Liquidise to a purée.Thicken this with a teaspoon of cornflour blended into 2 tablespoons of soya milk. Boil for 4 minutes to produce a thicker paste. Cool.

3. Place the egg whites in a clean bowl and add a pinch of salt. Beat the egg whites to a meringue and add the sugar 1 teaspoon at a time. Continue beating until all the sugar is used up and the egg whites form peaks when lifted with a whisk.

4. Fold the raspberry purée into this meringue very delicately but thouroughly. Fill the 6 moulds to the brim. Level up with a palette knife and make criss cross lines with a fork. Place the soufflés on a tray and bake at 220°C/425°F/Gas Mark 7 on the middle shelf for 20 minutes until well risen above

the rim. Serve hot immediately with a garnish of fresh raspberries or a compote of stewed peaches or pears.

ALMOND AND TOFU CURD SALAD

You could not find a richer protein fruit salad – nor a more nutritious one – than the one offered here.

4 portions • Preparation 15 minutes • Cooking 8 minutes

Ingredients	Metric	Imperial	American
Water	500ml	1 pint	2½ cups
Honey	50g	2 oz	¼ cup
Almonds, flaked	75g	3 oz	⅓ cup
Soya milk	150ml	¼ pint	⅔ cup
Agar powder	50g	2 oz	¼ cup
Sunflower oil	25ml	1 fl oz	1½ tbsp
Assorted fruit, e.g. apples, pears, melon, orange, etc.	450g	1 lb	4 cups
Almond curd			
Tofu	285ml	10 oz	2½ cups

1. Boil the water and honey. Add the flaked almonds and cook for 2 minutes. Purée the mixture and reheat to boiling point. Add soya milk and sprinkle the agar powder in and the almond curd. Cook for 10 minutes to dissolve it. Grease a shallow tray with oil and pour the almond jelly in to cool and set.

2. When hardened, cut into squares and place in a salad bowl with the fruit and tofu. After marinading for about 20 minutes blend the fruit salad and serve in individual glasses decorated with orange slices and a sprig of fresh mint. Or serve in scooped out melon halves.

PEPPERMINT AND CAROB ICE CAKE

8 portions • Preparation 10 minutes • Freezing time 3 hours

Ingredients	**Metric**	**Imperial**	**American**
Peppermint mixture:			
Tofu block, chopped	285g	10 oz	2½ cups
Sunflower oil	50ml	2 fl oz	¼ cup
Honey	125g	5 oz	⅔ cup
Peppermint essence	6 drops	6 drops	6 drops
Carob Mixture:			
Carob bars	75g	3 oz	⅓ cup
Honey	75g	3 oz	⅓ cup
Tofu, chopped	150g	5 oz	1¼ cups
Brandy or rum	1 tbsp	1 tbsp	1 tbsp
Toasted almonds, flaked	15g	½ oz	1 tbsp
Sunflower oil	1 oz fl	25ml	2 tbsp

1 Place the peppermint ingredients in a liquidiser and blend to a purée. Line a greased charlotte mould with greaseproof paper. Heat the mixture to boiling point, cool and place in an ice cream tray and freeze for 3 hours.

2 In a saucepan melt the carob bars with the honey and chopped tofu. Add the brandy. Place in a liquidiser and purée. Reheat with toasted nuts for 1 minute. Cool and place in a shallow oiled ice cube tray. Freeze for 3 hours.

3 To make into a cake beat the green ice cream until smooth and line the bottom and sides of the charlotte mould with it. Place the carob ice cream in a bowl and beat to a smooth mixture to break down the ice crystals. Fill the centre of the mould with it. Refreeze the mould for 3 hours. When ready turn out on to a plate and decorate with a sprig of mint. Serve with macaroons.

Index